Deer Stalking in the Scottish Highlands

By
Various Authors

DEER STALKING AND HUNTING

Aside from man, all other carnivorous predators of adult deer have been hunted to extinction in Britain. In most cases the objective of deer stalking is to maintain a stable and healthy population of deer – in order to achieve this, a cull of about 30% of the population is required each year. This is not random however, and a population/age census will have been carried out each year by an *experienced* stalker to determine the age and sex profile of those to be culled. Injured or sick animals are given priority, then barren or very old animals, and after that, carefully selected animals. This will result in a balanced pyramid profile, with a few old animals of each sex at the top, with increasing numbers of each sex down to the yearlings at the bottom. The males at the top of the pyramid are sometimes seen as trophy animals though, attracting sportsmen who often pay substantial sums for shooting them. If population reduction is required, more females will be culled. If a population increase is required, only injured or sick animals will be culled.

A rifle will be used that complies with the minimum requirements of 'The Deer Act' in calibre and ballistic performance. There are differences in the law between Scotland, England and Wales, and popular calibres are .243, .270, .303, .308, 6.5x55mm, .25-06, and .30-06. In recent times the use of sound moderators ("silencers") has greatly increased, partly for reasons of health, and partly as a safety measure.

"Deer stalking" is a British term for the stealthy pursuit of deer on foot, for sport, numerical control, or food. Deer are usually shot with a high powered rifle, though woodland stalking with bow or crossbow is also popular in some countries where this practice is allowed. While the expression "deer stalking" is widely used among British and Irish sportsmen to signify almost all forms of sporting deer shooting, the term is replaced in North American sporting usage by "deer *hunting*." This expression *deer hunting* is a term that in Britain and Ireland has historically been reserved *exclusively* for the sporting pursuit of deer with scent hounds, with unarmed followers typically on horseback. The practice of hunting with hounds (other than using two hounds to flush deer to be shot by waiting marksmen), has been banned in the UK since 2005. Prior to that there were several packs of staghounds hunting wild red deer of both sexes on or around Exmoor. This practice continued until 1997, when they were disbanded, alongside the *New Forest Buckhounds* who hunted fallow deer bucks in the New Forest.

Pre-twentieth century, there were several packs of staghounds hunting "carted deer" in England and Ireland. Carted deer were Red deer kept in captivity for the sole purpose of being hunted and recaptured without harm. Carted deer that escaped recapture sometimes became the source of wild populations. For example the red deer of

Thetford Chase originated with deer left out by the *Norwich Staghounds*.

The way in which the red deer were traditionally hunted was for a hunt servant called the "harbourer" to follow the intended quarry to the wood where it lay up for the night. In the morning before the meet the harbourer would carefully examine the perimeter of the wood to ensure that the stag had not left. He then reported to the Master, and the Huntsman would take about six hounds called the "tufters" into the wood and rouse the intended quarry whilst separating it from any other deer that might be in the wood. This having been achieved, the tufters were called off, their work being done for the day, and the main pack were brought out and laid on the scent of the stag – which by now had a good start. After an often protracted chase the stag would become exhausted and eventually, would be shot at close range by one of the hunt servants.

The use of the term "stalking" serves to denote the extreme stealth and wariness which are often necessary when approaching wild deer in their natural habitats. Scottish deer stalking is often done under the guidance of a stalker or a gillie; a resident expert. Deer stalking is virtually the only form of control, or culling, for the six wild or feral species of deer at large in the UK. The six species are Red Deer, Roe Deer, Fallow Deer, Sika Deer, Muntjac and Chinese Water Deer and there have never been more deer at large, or more widely distributed in the UK than there are today.

The first two species are indigenous although new populations have appeared after deliberate releases and escapes from parks or farms. A result of this is that both Red Deer and Roe Deer are now present in several parts of Wales, a country from which both had been absent as wild animals for several centuries. Fallow Deer have been at large in many parts of the UK for at least 1,000 years, added to by more recent escapes, but the other three species have solely originated from ornamental collections and deer farms, principally from Woburn Abbey, escaping through damaged fences or sometimes by deliberate release. A number of deer and wild boar also escaped in southern England following damage to fences by the hurricane of 1987.

Apart from the stalking of Red and Sika Deer on the open hillsides of Scotland, Ireland and the Lake District (which takes place in daylight), most deer stalking takes place in the first and last two hours of daylight – when wild deer are most active. Trophy antlers are measured by one of several scoring systems used to compare the relative merits of the heads. In Europe (including the UK) the Conseil International du Chasse (CIC) system is used, in America it is either the Boone & Crockett or Safari Club International (SCI), and in Australasia the Douglas system is used.

This book has been reprinted for its historical value and cultural significance, as well as its reading pleasure. Much of the practical information regarding the ancient sport of deer stalking and hunting, which dates back thousands (even tens of thousands) of years, is still of interest today – and we hope, is of benefit to the current reader.

John Ross, F.S.A. Scot.

Deerstalking
in the Scottish Highlands

By JOHN ROSS, F.S.A., Scot.

Chleirach d' an leabhair bhain,
   Gu chun a tha 'n sgoile soillear,
Cha 'n eil Ifrinn aite co donna
Ma bhios con a's fiadh anna.
                    —OSSIAN

O! Holy Priest, with sacred lore,
   To whom all mysteries are clear,
Hell cannot have such ills in store,
   If it contains both dogs and deer.

THE lure of the Scottish Highlands can be somewhat uncomfortably realised by any doubting visitor at the great London railway stations — Euston, St. Pancras, or King's Cross—in the first weeks of August or even before then at Perth—the gateway of the Grampians — the guardian mountains that defied the might of Rome, and behind whose barriers have been retained traditions and characteristics of race and language that have endowed these hills and valleys with world-wide fame. Is it the country itself with its varied and rugged scenery, or the wild animals that still rove untamed in their fastnesses of mountain and moor, or the people blended of Celt and Saxon and Viking, that have dowered this part of the island with such associations of sport and romance? Perchance it may be all three, for here the red deer still show their stately forms on the sky-line of lofty hills or in the bracken-clad recesses of remote corries, near boisterous torrents that pursue their rough and tortuous course to the sea,

A

while from the remote valley below can be heard the strains of the bagpipes played by a kilted Highlander proudly arrayed in the tartan that his broadsword has made known in every quarter of the globe, from the mud fields of Flanders to the jungles of Cathay.

Considering its extent, this part of Scotland, the most sparsely inhabited, and the most mountainous area in Great Britain, has many remarkable features. Its mountains ascend from the coast in masses of land broken by countless valleys, lochs, and streams, to an altitude of over 4000 feet. In Ross-shire alone there are 80 hills over 3000 feet high. The firths, or sea inlets penetrate the land so far and so often, especially in the precipitous West, that in no part is the sea too far distant to be reached on foot by a hardened deer-stalker in the span of a summer's day. This day indeed becomes long in the time of the summer solstice, and mountaineers have maintained that they have seen on peaks in Sutherland, the sun sinking in his glory in the West while the streaks of dawn appeared in the East. I myself have read my newspaper at midnight in midsummer (and not "legal summer" time at that) in my native county of Caithness. The climate too, in Autumn is as a rule remarkably invigorating, with beautiful skies and refreshing scenes. Though the Shetland Isles are in the same latitude as the South of Greenland and the north of Labrador, thanks to the Gulf Stream, all the ports of Britain are free of ice all the year round. Thus it happens that the climate of this small island is unique, and one can understand travellers who have visited every quarter of the globe, when they affirm that the climate of the Highlands at its best, is unsurpassed. This is of course in spite of its rain and its mists, which may often hang about the mountains and baulk the deer-stalkers of many a good day's sport. The late Duke of Sutherland, who was a great traveller and loved especially the Canadian plains and the Rockies, was known to point to Glen Dhu from Kyle Sku in the west of Sutherland, and to declare with fervour that it was the finest view he had ever seen in the world.   There in the dim vista, the fiords push their sinuous arms into the land, while the crests of the mighty mountains, clad in their Autumn coat of heather, gradually become merged in the mists above. It is amid these hills and these recesses that the deer roam at will, and it is on these moors that the grouse have their natural home. While sheep, too, can feed for most part of the year in these lofty uplands, the deer, one feels, are the natural inhabitants, just as the trout are the denizens of the countless lochs that dot the landscape.

It must not be overlooked that the many islands to the West, once part of the mainland, but now cut off by deep and stormy channels, are also great haunts of the deer. Lewis, Skye, and Mull are homes of the red deer famed in Ossian's songs, as also are other isles, especially Jura.   These isles inspired the muse of Scott, and also of his friend John Leyden, the famous traveller and linguist, as can be seen from the following reference in "The Lord of the Isles :" —

> " And verdant Islay called her host
> And the Clans of Jura's rugged coast
>   Lord Ronald's call obey,
> And Scarba's Isle, whose tortured shore
> Still rings to Corrievreken's roar,
>   And lonely Colonsay.
> Scenes sung by him who sings no more !
> His bright and brief career is o'er,
>   And mute his tuneful strains ;
> Quenched is his lamp of varied lore,
> That loved the light of song to pour;
> A distant and a deadly shore,
>   Has Leyden's cold remains ! "

Such is the configuration of the land, and it no doubt had its influence on the people. The clans with their feuds and their forays, their retention of their ancient habits and freedom in their mountain homes, their language with its fine literature, their loyalty to the Stuart cause and the wanderings of Prince Charlie —"whom there was none to betray" for £30,000, the price placed on his head, though hundreds amid the hills and isles knew his haunts for months—and the fighting qualities of the Highland regiments have also played their part in touching the bens and the glens with that halo of romance which human activities and human sufferings alone can bestow.

The changing conditions of the country also brought a glamour to this comparatively remote land. In the early days of Britain, the country was full of game and the hunter had plenty of scope. As the population increased, and towns and villages sprang up, the game here as elsewhere diminished until only on the high hills and remote areas of the north could the animals be found in their natural surroundings. The hunting instincts of the people, however, remained, and while the opportunities ceased to gratify this desire, other modes of sport developed as a substitute which have probably made this country in that respect unique in the annals of peoples. As is pointed out in the article on Empire Building, the instincts of the hunter attracted many men to travel and exploration.

Kingsley the author of " Westward Ho," describes in his poem, " The Outlaw," the instinctive lure of the chase in the blood of the youth who could not repress his love of the open air and its freedom :—

" I wadna be a clerk, mither, to bide aye ben
Scrabbling ower the sheets o' parchment with a weary, weary pen ;
Looking through the lang stane windows at a narrow strip o' sky,
Like a laverock in a withy cage, until I pine away and die.

And so it was that I won the heart to wander far and near
Caring neither for land nor lassie but the bonny dun deer,
So I'm aff and away to the muirs, mither, to hunt the deer,

Ranging far frae frowning faces and the douce folk here,
Crawling up through burn and bracken, louping down the screes,
Looking up frae craig and headland drinking up the summer breeze.

Oh ! the wafts o' heather honey, and the music o' the brae,
As I watch the great harts feeding, nearer, nearer a' the day,
Oh ! to hear the eagle screaming, sweeping, ringing round the sky,
The live-long night on the black hill sides where the dun deer lie."

Perhaps after all, this is the lure and the kernel of the truth. What can be more delightful, than a day among the heather clad hills in pursuit of the wary stag ? The cool bracing air with the mountain peaks in the distance, their lower reaches clad with trees, the undulating ground with many recesses that have to be carefully crossed with every precaution against being seen, heard, or scented, all combine to give a feeling of keenness and alertness that banish worry and memories of the artificial life of the town. Care has to be taken when the crest is being reached to prevent the keen-eyed and keen-scenting deer from being disturbed until the trained observer with his glasses scans the distant ground. Then if a good head is spotted, the gradual retreat, the stealthy crawl, through crag and heath and moss, the anxiety about the direction or variations of the wind, until a favourable position is reached for the tremulous shot, and then—even if it be a miss, the quest has not been in vain. After all there is some truth in Byron's cynical lines :—

" Tis an old saying, time approves it true,
    And those who know it best deplore it most,
When all is won that one desires to woo
    The paltry prize is hardly worth the cost."

The trophy is as often as not valued for the memories of the struggle and the toil to secure it, and for the success of the effort rather than for its intrinsic worth, and deep down in his soul, the huntsman probably is glad his quarry escaped.

THE DEATH OF THE THIRTEEN-POINTER.

The art and charm of deer-stalking have been so frequently described by abler pens than mine, and are being so well depicted in later chapters in this book that I do not propose to attempt it. One of the finest writers on the subject, whose volume on " Deer-stalking and other sport in the Highlands " is an authoritative work, was Mr Augustus Grimble, who, on hearing of this projected volume, wrote to me to express his interest ; and my co-editor, Mr Hugh Gunn and I had the pleasure of talking with him on the subject of deer-stalking only three weeks before his lamented death in February, 1925. He regretted that he would not be able to contribute an article himself owing to the state of his health, but he expressed a wish that any extracts from his work might be used, and it was only his unexpected death that has prevented the publication of an autographed foreword by the distinguished author himself.

I have pleasure accordingly in quoting the following extract from his book, with my tribute to the memory of a real sportsman. It relates to the death of a thirteen-pointer :—

" Angus was downright bloodthirsty that day, for, as we finished a hasty lunch, he jumped to his feet, saying—" Well, sir, all last season no one rifle could get more than three beasts in a day to himself, but I think we shall manage to beat that now, so we'll start whenever you're ready."

Nothing loth, I was on my legs at once, but in vain corrie after corrie was searched, for not another beast could we see, while by about half-past four we had explored all the likeliest places and were reduced to turning back. At this Angus was quite depressed, but I could not in any way share his feelings, for three stags in one day should surely be sufficient, while I was even more than content. As we made for home, Angus spied all the ground over again, but it was of no use, and we at last arrived at the edge of the range of the forest hills.

From where we stood we could see the lodge, a speck in the distance, while Dyke's boat was still fishing the loch, some three thousand feet below us. It was such a pretty scene of hill country that we were tempted to rest, before commencing the long descent so trying to the knees, so we sat down at a spring and lighted our pipes, to repose awhile. Once again Angus pulled out his glass, and all feelings of fatigue left me as he said, " May be, sir, we shall get a fourth beast for I can see a small stag feeding on the top of the inch burn, though I doubt if the daylight will last us."

I took the glass out of his hand, and soon found the staggie which was such a small beastie that I at once began to consider whether after the good day we had had, it would not be more sportsmanlike to leave him in peace. On imparting these sentiments to Angus, I found he had set his heart on making up the four beasts, while he also told me the stag was bigger than his horns indicated, so I took another peep to inspect him afresh, when he made a sudden bolt in evident alarm, while over the sky-line in angry pursuit there came a splendid stag with a grand head. Nearly certain I could count royal points I was about to disclaim my discovery to Angus, when it flashed across my mind how pushed we were for time, and as with all his skill, he was yet a very excitable man, I feared it might make him rush if he suddenly heard of the presence of such a grand beast, so I kept my own counsel, and quickly shutting up his glass, I handed it back, while remarking quite unconcernedly " Well, Angus, if you wish to get up to him in time to see to shoot it must be a case of running, so go ahead as fast as you like."

Go, indeed, he did, but as it was down hill for a mile, I managed to live with him till the ascent began, and then Angus, like a gentleman, made the pace less severe, while as he came to the top of the hill over which we expected to find our quarry, he had the wisdom to reduce it almost to a crawl, and by the time the summit was reached I had quite recovered my wind.

On hands and knees we crossed the sky-line, while yard by yard the precipitous sides of the Inch burn were searched, and possibly disappointed at finding our deer had probably fed nearer to the foot of the very steep hill. A worse place for a shot could not be imagined, and Angus whispered to me that the last three stags killed here had all been smashed to bits by rolling down the hillside after receiving the bullet.

There was nothing for it but to follow our quarry, so feet first and flat on our sides we commenced the descent, only soon to sight the back of a small stag. As long as he fed we slithered nearer to him ; the moment he lifted his head we were as immovable as the big stones around us. At length we were within a long shot of this staggie, while to my dismay nothing of the big fellow could be seen, and it became uncertain whether our quarry was lower down the hill, or hidden from our view by a projecting spur of rock. Just for fun, with no intention of firing, I put the rifle to my shoulder, when to my surprise Angus' long arm glided round me and depressed the muzzle to the earth, while a hurried whisper came to my ear, " there is another one just a wee bit better."

Now as I also knew there was another and a very much better one, I chuckled to myself at the thought of the surprise it would be to Angus, if we succeeded in killing the royal. The situation was however, getting critical and would speedily have to be decided, for it was growing dusk so rapidly that unless the small stag would kindly move out of the way it would be impossible to make a further advance without letting him into the secret of our presence, and in that case he would be certain to impart his discovery to his friends below.

For some precious minutes we remained immovable, while hoping the little beast would take himself off, but he kept on placidly browsing, while each mouthful he took was accompanied on our part by anything but blessings on his head. Dusker and dusker it grew, and matters began to look very black ; so much so, that I thought of confiding all about the royal to Angus, with the view of taking hurried counsel and attempting some rush or daring manoeuvre. My own idea was to put the rifle at full cock, and then with fingers just set between hammers and strikers, to make a dash down hill, trusting to luck to get near enough to the big stag to take a shot before he could run out of range. As I turned to whisper my plans, I saw two other good sized stags coming up from the base of the hill, to join the party above them, for in addition to the small stag with the big one there were also a lot of hinds. Angus had seen them too, and whispered to me in sad despairing accents, ' Hech, sir, if it were but later in the season the other stag would soon put them awa, and show us where he was.' As he finished speaking the two intruders came to a halt, while the provoking little staggie that had delayed our advance disappeared with a caper ; then the next second we heard the clatter, the thud, and the rush of a heavy beast in his gallop accompanied by snorts of rage and defiance, while the two stags in the distance turned to fly.

It was clear that the sounds we heard, came from behind the projecting rock, so now our anxiety was as to whether the stag would continue his pursuit far enough down the hill to bring himself to our view. It was clear if he did put in an appearance we should be absolutely in full view of each other, so the full-cocked rifle was already at my shoulder as, after a few seconds of suspense, he bounded into sight about a hundred yards below me. He came thundering down the hill fairly broadside on, and excited as I was, it was yet impossible to help admiring the spectacle, for though we were as motionless as the rocks around us, he ' picked us up ' in an instant, and brought himself to a sudden halt with his fore legs planted stiff and wide in front of him, with his head turned directly

B

on us. We were equally quick to see we were detected, and realised that in another second he would bolt down-hill to be lost to view. Alas ! for him that second of hesitation was his death warrant, for the rifle spoke in the very nick of time, and he fell to all appearance stone dead. Quickly lowering the hammer of the left barrel, and putting the stop on, we dashed down-hill with lengthy leaps to where he lay, only to reach him just as the sinewy hind legs began to kick in vigorous convulsions ; on to one of them Angus flung himself, while I seized his horns and fixed his head to the earth, so thus between us we held him till the knife could be got at. A few minutes later the gallant stag lay prone on the now nearly dark hillside, and we began to realise the good luck that had befallen us, for at our feet was a splendid thirteen-pointer, which next day, without heart or liver, scaled seventeen stone.

Then I turned mockingly to Angus while saying, "Well, now what do you think of my little stag ? I saw him when you told me to take a look at the small one, but I kept it dark, to give you a pleasant surprise." The reply came—" Hech, sir, but its just the verra same stag I was hoping to get you a chance at. You see, sir, it was like this—I hae so often seen the sicht of such a grand beast as this mak my gentlemen all o'er of a tremble, that I just telled ye it was but a staggie we were after ; but surely sir, ye did not see him too, for he went out of sicht before I passed you my glass."

To this I answered, " Yes, Angus, but he came back again, and so I kept the matter dark, for I, too, have sometimes seen the sight of such a splendid stag make the best of stalkers rush, especially when he had to do his work against time ; so we can each laugh at the other and cry quits over our thirteen-pointer. So now for a taste of Glenlivet before we drag him down the hill."

A Fine Royal   Photo by Chas. Reid

"The Hunter Home from the Hill"   Photo by Chas. Reid

A Herd in Sanctuary   Photo by Chas. Reid

Hinds shot at Glencarron
(Photo reproduced by permission of Lady Evelyn Cobbold)

The Home of the Deer.

The area of the Scottish Deer Forests—and that means practically all in Britain—would far from equal that of the South African or New Zealand Game Reserves, and would be lost in the vast expanse of the Great National Parks of Canada which have been set aside for all time in their primeval beauty and wildness with the entire plant and animal life, for the use of the Canadian people. Yet these reserves, valuable as they are, cannot compare with the variety of the interest of the Highland hills. The latter have all the glamour of mountain and valley, loch and sea, and unique conditions of climate, and with the multitudinous turmoil of London's millions of inhabitants and its world-visitors within a journey of a few hours. It is the touch of human life that brings glamour to the fairest scene.

The writer has not been privileged to hunt big game beyond his native heath, but his interest in all forms of wild animal hunting is thereby all the greater. If there were more animals of a savage nature still surviving in Britain, it is probable that the stag would not occupy such a leading place. That he is, however, of high sporting interest to men who have shot big game all over the world will be realised, from the assurance of Dr Kingsley, the brother of the author of " Westward Ho." After shooting big game all over the world from the wolf to the buffalo and the elk, " I vow," he wrote " that all said and done I think that stalking an educated stag in a Highland corrie is the most exquisitely delicious sport that I have ever tried. . . . . Half past five the rain pattering against the window panes and the birches outside swishing and rasping against the walls with a vehemence that tells of a rattling sou-wester. Dark grey mist driving past only permitting us to see fifty yards of the lake, lead coloured, flecked with foam and long white foaming streaks like a tide way. To dress or not to dress! To turn out and drive seven miles in the teeth of the storm and find our horizon capable of being touched with the point of a ramrod when we reach the stalking ground, or to turn in under the warm bed clothes again, to wake up at nine o'clock with a guilty conscience to the reality of a glorious morning, so clear and bright after the rain that I can almost count the stones on the top of Ben Clebrig—to be told that the household is aweary of mutton and languish for venison—to find the river in full spate and salmon impossibilities—to have one's health tenderly inquired after by Donald ?—Never ! Tub-sleep-dispeller ! welcome ! and to break-fast at six with a Sutherland appetite ! "

Then follows the description of the journey to the forest, and the talk with the ghillies and the inevitable reference to Sir Robert Gordon, who wrote in the seventeenth century about the " vert and venaison " of the County of Sutherland. " All these forests and schases," writes Sir Robert " are very profitable for feeding for bestiall and delectable for hunting. They are full of reid deer, roes, woulffs, foxes, wyld catts, brocks, skuyrells, whittrets, weasels, otters, martrixes, hares, and foumarts. In these fforests, and in all this pro-vince, ther is great store of partridges, pluviers, capercaleys, blackcoaks, mure fowls, heth-hens, swanes, bewters, turtle-doves, herons, dowes, steares or starlings, lair-igig, or knag, (which is a fowl like unto a parokeet or parrot, which makes place for nest with her beek in the oak-tree) duke, draig, widgeon, teale, wildgoose, ringoose, gouls, wharps, shot wharps, woodcocks, larkes, sparrows, snyps, blackbuirds, and all other kinds of wild-fowl, and birds which are to be had in any part of this kingdom."

I quote this catalogue of wild things with patriotic pride in the prolific offspring of my native hills ! Perhaps with all this wild life about, the stag was not so personally vigilant in the days of old, when he had so many associates in his mountain fastnesses. Now the stalker maligns the grouse because its warning " whirr " tells the monarch of the glen that his foe is near. What would he have said to the manifold manifestations of life that formerly enlivened the silence of the hills ?

THE PASSING OF THE LAST LONE WOLF.

The reference to wolves by Sir Robert Gordon may appropriately permit me to recall that the last wolf in Britain was killed in Lothbeg, in Sutherlandshire, about the year 1700. It was thought that after the slaughter of the two full-grown and two young wolves in one day in the Reay country by a Mackay, that these destructive animals were exterminated, but some nocturnal ravages amongst the flocks in Loth, showed that some still existed. It so happened that a man named Polson, an expert hunter himself, with his son and another boy in following up the search for the lair of the wolves, discovered a narrow entrance to a cave which he suspected was the home of these animals. The two boys managed to squeeze through the entrance to the cavern below, and found five or six lively wolf cubs with the debris of recent meals. They informed Polson, and he told them to destroy the cubs, and hurry out again. In his anxiety to see what was happening he pushed his head into the entrance, and thus shut out the light. They told him not to obstruct the light, and he stepped a few paces aside. Scarcely had he done so than he heard the feeble howls of the whelps as they were attacked, and to his horror, saw a furious full-grown wolf, evidently the mother, outside the entrance preparing to dash into the cave. He was just in time to catch her tail as she was half-way into the entrance in which she could not turn. Polson was able by exerting his full strength to keep her from entering the den. The struggle continued in silence until Polson finally overcame the wolf by stabs from the dirk which he was fortunately able to draw from its sheath. Meanwhile the lads were proceeding with the work of destruction as best they could in their dark retreat until the son shouted to his struggling father from the depths below, " What is keeping the light away " ? The father's reply is now a proverb in its native Gaelic :—" If the root of the tail breaks you will soon know." The wolf and her dead whelps were brought home as trophies, and a stone recently erected by the Duke of Portland commemorates the historic event.*

THE STAG AT BAY.

A very interesting chapter could be written about the wild animals of the Highlands, many of which are classed as vermin owing to their destructive habits. Space, however, will not permit apart from the restrictions of this volume to the red deer and other sporting big game. Stalking has not been the only way of " chasing " the red deer, and the hunting of the deer of Exmoor by horsemen and with hounds is a survival of this ancient form of " venerie " which at one time prevailed all over the country. Sir Samuel Baker, one of the greatest hunters of big game that ever lived,† records an interesting hunt in which he with the aid of dogs succeeded in bringing a stag to bay in the mountains of Atholl. Let the great Nimrod tell it in his own inimitable way :—

" There is hardly a more sporting sight than a stag at bay, but as the dogs are trained simply to follow a wounded deer until it stands, when the baying of the hounds will attract the attention of the far distant men; the termination of the hunt is a tame affair, as the deer is shot directly the rifle arrives upon the scene. About thirty-two years have passed away (1890) since we discussed the question whether the deer hounds at Blair would seize a stag if it was considered necessary. Most persons who have the training of the dogs thought not. The Duke of Atholl inclined to that opinion. On the other side I thought they would, provided that no rifles were taken out and the dogs should see that the stag was to be tackled at close quarters with the knife. There never was a

---

* This story of the last wolf is related by Scope in his "Deerstalking in the Highlands."

† *Wild Beasts and Their Ways*, by Sir Samuel Baker. MacMillan & Co. 2 vols. 1890.

TO MARK THE PLACE NEAR WHICH,
(ACCORDING TO SCROPE'S "ART OF DEERSTALKING")
THE LAST WOLF IN SUTHERLAND
WAS KILLED
BY THE HUNTER, POLSON,
IN OR ABOUT THE YEAR 1700,
THIS STONE WAS ERECTED BY
HIS GRACE THE DUKE OF PORTLAND, K.G.,
A.D. 1924.

The Lone Sheiling Photo by Chas. Reid

Highland Cattle at Home Photo by Chas. Reid

keener sportsman than his Grace the Duke of Atholl, and he was good enough to consent to a trial.   The arguments had interested the ladies of the party, and it was arranged that I might select any two of the deer hounds, and hunt down a fresh stag, run it to bay, and kill it with a knife.   To myself the affair appeared exceedingly simple, as I had been accustomed to this kind of hunting for many years in the mountains of Ceylon, but others disbelieved that the two hounds would bring a fresh deer to bay, as they had always been accustomed to follow animals that were wounded.   By the advice of the head forester, Sandy MacCarra, I chose my old friend Oscar, and another hound whose name I have forgotten.

We were a large party, and we met at the Forest Lodge about ten miles from the Castle, in the middle of Glen Tilt.   There are few glens in the Highlands more picturesque.   The road from Blair Castle passes through lovely woods bordering the impetuous stream that rushes wildly through contracted passes hemmed in by opposing rocks.   Sometimes it is girt by stony cliffs half concealed by lichens, other portions of the face combine every shade of colouring in vivid tints.   The mountain ash with clusters of scarlet berries overhangs the rocks in rich profusion of both fruit and foliage until the length of the open glen is reached beyond the limit of the woods.

This is a well-known resort of tourists, and nothing can exceed the wild beauty of the scene, when about the middle of September, the autumnal tints have ornamented every leaf with peculiar brightness.   Although we have emerged from the main woods, there are clumps of weeping birch with its silver bark and golden leaves, and rowan thickets bending over the rapid river, now and then reflected in the calm surface of a deep pool, where the salmon are lying waiting for a flood.   This kind of rough scenery continues throughout the glen, the narrow bottom occupied by the river bordered by a good road while the mountains rise upon either side and form the Grampian Hills.

The afternoon was perfect : all that was required was game.

Certainly the presence of many ladies brought us luck, for after scanning in vain a long expanse of country, we were suddenly delighted by the almost magical appearance of a stag : he had been lying down behind a large rock, a little more than half way up the hill face. He now stood regarding the carriages, and our large party, which included the keepers, and the two hounds from Forest Lodge. The stag was about 1000 yards distant. I was only afraid that he would commence a trot up the hill, and disappear above the sky-line, but fortunately we were upon the main road upon which the deer were accustomed to regard passengers (although few) who did not interfere in any manner with their domain. It was therefore decided that the party should turn back and drive for about a mile on the Castle side of Forest Lodge while I should walk up until I should be out of the deer's sight. I could then discover a favourable position for ascending the hill and coming down from above upon the stag. This was an excellent arrangement. The party turned back, while I continued on my way, accompanied by two of the hillmen and the dogs.

It did not take us long to climb the hill and we found ourselves upon the well known desolate extent of heather, sloping always upward although we had reached what from below appeared to be the summit. There were a few hinds within view and some young harts, but they were not in a position to disturb the stag, who was far away out of sight, being on our left well below upon the hill face.

There was neither caution nor science required, therefore we made a quick advance, marching parallel with the glen about a quarter of a mile on the right of the incline above the Tilt.

When arrived at the position which I had roughly calculated as above the spot where we had seen the stag we turned to our left and came downwards until we were in sight of Glen Tilt, and we could see the carriages with our entire party waiting on the road upon our right. The deer was not in sight. This was exceedingly awkward as it looked as though he had suspected danger and had departed.

My men did not think so. They thought that he had again lain down when the carriages turned and were lost to view. It was the party which had disturbed him, therefore he had again reposed when the party had gone. In this opinion, I agreed. We accordingly held the dogs in readiness to slip immediately, and the ghillie led the way. We were not kept many minutes in suspense : there was no doubt that the stag was lying down, as he suddenly sprang up from the heather and the broken surface of the hill face.

This must have been a lovely sight from the carriages, although rather far from the unassisted eye. For a few seconds the stag took up the hill, but the hounds ran cunning and cut him off : he then took a straight course along the face towards the direction where the carriages were waiting below. The hounds were going madly, and were gaining on him. I now felt certain that he could not breast the hill at such a pace, therefore, instead of following over the rough ground, we made all speed direct for the bottom to gain the level road. It did not take long to reach the welcome solid footing and away we went, as hard as we could go, along the road towards the direction of the carriages. As we drew near, we could see the hunt. The deer had passed the spot where our party was in waiting, but he now turned down the hill towards the river with the two dogs within a few yards of his heels. Presently we lost sight of everything : we rushed forward, passed the carriages, which were empty, as everybody had joined in the hunt, and after running about a quarter of a mile down the road, we heard the bay and shortly arrived at the spot where the stag was standing in the middle of a rapid and the hounds were baying from the bank. No doubt the hounds expected to hear the crack of a rifle, and to see the gallant stag totter and fall in the foaming river, according to their old experiences. However, they were not long in doubt. Patting both the excited hounds upon the back, and giving them a

C

loud halloo, I jumped into the water, which was hardly more than hip deep, but the stream was very rapid. The stag, upon seeing my advance, ran down the bed of the river, and halted again after a short run of 50-60 yards. The two keepers had followed me and Oscar, and his companion no longer thought of baying from the bank but being carried forward by the torrent, together with ourselves, were met by the stag with lowered antlers. I never saw dogs behave better, although for a moment one was beneath the water. Oscar was hanging to the ear, I caught hold of the horn to assist the dog, and at the same moment the other hound was holding by the throat. The knife had made its thrust, behind the shoulder, and the two ghillies were holding fast, by the horns, to prevent the torrent from carrying away the dying animal. This had been a pretty course which did not last long, but it was properly managed, and in my opinion, ten times better sport than shooting a deer at bay."

This incident, so graphically recorded by one of the greatest of big game hunters, recalls to my mind the first occasion upon which I made the acquaintance of the red deer, and an acquaintance at close quarters it indeed proved to be. As a lad in my early teens, I spent a holiday in the beauty spot of Caithness, Berriedale, a sporting estate belonging to the Duke of Portland. Naturally I took a boy's eager interest in all that pertained to sport, and counted it a great piece of good fortune to be allowed to take part in the search for a wounded stag which had escaped the stalkers the previous day. It was believed that he had taken refuge in a belt of wood fringing the Berriedale river, and a number of beaters were sent into the wood. My part was to watch on the outskirts of the wood with Roy (I think that was his name), a crafty old collie whose ideas on deer-stalking methods were based upon his proper profession of looking after sheep. I had not long to wait, for a tug at the leash showed that Roy was on the alert, and sure enough the antlers of a royal stag appeared above the under-

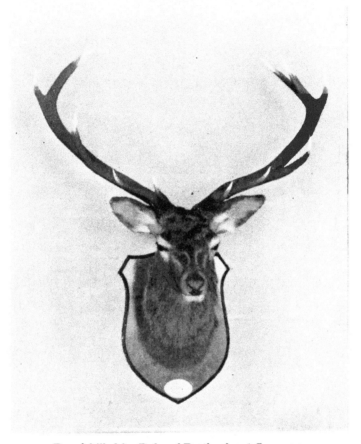

Royal killed by Duke of Portland, 1st Sep., 1924
Weight 20 st.   Width of Horn 30½ ins.   Thickness 5⅛ ins.

The Duke of Portland and Shooting Party at Langwell

growth and a moment later the stag himself, wounded in the ribs, where a dull stain of clotted blood told its own tale.

My instructions were to slip the collie as soon as I saw the stag, and this I did.   Roy was off like a shot, the stag having a matter of thirty yards start.   I had a clear view of the chase, which was uphill for some three or four hundred yards, the deer making a great pace in spite of his wound, with Roy gradually overhauling him.   Just on the summit of the hill Roy caught up and rounded his quarry, exercising all his customary arts of intimidation. Roy's instinct was to bring him back to where he found him. The stag turned about and the pair came racing towards me again, Roy now making no attempt to overtake the stag, though he could easily have done so.

For a short while they were lost in a hollow, then they appeared making towards the river.   The stag headed right on until it reached the water, into which he plunged, and standing knee-deep turned at bay, lowering his antlers as though to defy Roy. There is not the least doubt he could, wounded as he was, have tossed Roy yards away had he ventured near him ; but the collie was wise in his day and generation, and, feeling that his particular work had been done, and that it was up to others to carry on, he stood on the bank, with his tongue lolling out of his mouth.

The picture of the stag standing there at bay, lingers in my mind with all the vividness of boyhood's memories, and with its background of stream and forest it would be a fit subject for any artist's pencil.   One could not but admire his indomitable pluck, and wonder that he could have put forth such an effort when fatally wounded.   The scene recalls the familiar passage from " As You Like It," where the melancholy Jaques

> " . . . . lay along
> Under an oak whose antique root peeps out
> Upon the brook that brawls along this wood,

> To the which place a poor sequestered stag,
>   Which from the hunter's wound had ta'en a hurt.
>   Did come to languish."

But the gallant animal was not to remain long in pain, for a shot rang out—from close range and mercifully accurate—and he collapsed in the stream, dead instantaneously.

THE ELUSIVE HIND.

The hind is undoubtedly one of the most interesting and beautiful creatures in the animal world, not even excepting her lord and master the stag. If the terms " form divine " and " poetry of motion " can be applied to any creature the hind has first claim upon them. In movement, whether walking, trotting or galloping, her action is perfect. She is more alert in every sense than the stag, who is well aware of this, as when accompanied by his harem of anything up to fifteen hinds, he knows he can safely browse or rest when protected by such trustworthy outposts. The hinds' sense of smell and hearing are intensely acute, and when suddenly alarmed she barks loudly to warn the other members of the herd. Deer-stalkers well know how difficult it is to get within shooting distance of a stag when in the company of hinds.

As a mother the hind has few equals, and has been known to beat off eagles and foxes in defence of her calf. When she feels she requires relaxation from maternal duties, and is in the mood for a scamper with the other hinds of the herd, she carefully selects cover for her calf, and by some means known only to herself, communicates to the youngster that he must remain there till she returns, and these instructions he implicitly obeys even though she is away for hours.

There is no authentic record of a hind having had more than one calf at a time, though occasionally they have been seen suckling the year old and the baby at the same time.

December and January are the two months hinds are at their best, and in my opinion stalking the hind is far and away more difficult and consequently more interesting than stalking the stag. I suppose it is chiefly owing to weather conditions that proprietors and lessees of deer forests do not take more interest in this sport than is generally the case. As a rule they leave the task of thinning down the hinds to their keepers and stalkers.

Some Natural History Notes.

The animal kingdom may popularly be divided into three distinct groups :—

1. Graminivorous, subsisting entirely on vegetation.
2. Omnivorous, subsisting partly on flesh and fish and vegetation.
3. Carnivorous, subsisting entirely on flesh and blood.

It is obvious that these were created in the above order, as No. 2, could not exist without No. 1, and No. 3 could not exist without Nos. 1 and 2.

As far as I am aware there is no record of any beast of prey having horns, antlers, tusks, or hooves. They are consequently completely dependent upon teeth and claw for attack and defence.

On the other hand the prey of carnivorous animals have natural protections of one kind or another. Cattle, buffalo and branches of the bovidae and antelope families have horns, deer have antlers, elephants and wild pigs have tusks, while nearly all the members of the two first species have hooves. Most of them can use their hooves with deadly effect, and a blow from the hoof of a hind will split the skull of a man. The buffalo is more than a match for any beast of prey if attacked single-handed, and as a rule he is only attacked by his enemies in pairs or groups. Even the domestic cow in defence of her offspring has been known to beat off a lion, while a wild boar in a fight with the lion or tiger is more than a match for either.

With regard to the stag, naturalists have never yet satisfactorily answered the questions as to why they have antlers, and why they shed these annually. Many writers assert that the antlers are provided to enable the stags to fight each other during the rutting season, but Mother Nature never yet equipped any of her offspring with weapons for settling domestic quarrels, and it does not seem reasonable to expect that she made an exception in the case of the deer family. The number of fights between stags are, taking the number of these animals into consideration, comparatively few, and there can be little doubt that the antlers were provided as a protection against the onslaught of their natural enemies. The skin of no beast of prey is invulnerable to the brow tines of a charging full-grown stag. The neck of the stag is very powerful, and the muscles and joints exceptionally tensile, and it would be exceedingly difficult for an enemy to get inside his guard unless he was taken by surprise. Wild beasts generally attack the throat or back of the neck, and antlers are obviously designed to protect these vulnerable parts from the enemy's onslaught. It may surprise most people to know that when a stag's head is thrown back the antlers cover most of his body. An experience I once had led me to the conclusion that one of the uses of antlers is to protect the neck and back from attack. A friend who was out with me in the Ardgoil Forest fired at a ten-pointer, but just grazed the skin above the small of the back. As soon as the stag felt the touch of the bullet his antlers were thrown back over the body, and he ran at least fifty yards before bringing them to the perpendicular. Did that movement come down to him from a remote ancestor when by a race-instinct he felt the claws of a leopard pierce his skin ?

It somewhat detracts from the theory that antlers were made for the purposes of racial war when it is known for a fact that in a fight the hummel stag is more than a match for his heavily-antlered antagonist. Many people are under the impression that

Killed by Duke of Portland
11th Oct., 1921
Weight 16 st.   Points 12
Width of Horn, inside 28 ins
Thickness 4¾ ins.

Killed by Duke of Portland
29th Sep., 1921
Weight 17 st. 8 lbs.   Points 14
Width of Horn, inside 31 ins.
Thickness 4¾ ins.

Killed by Duke of Portland
22nd Sep., 1913
Weight 20 st. 8 lbs.   Points 13
Width of Horn, inside 25 ins.
Thickness 5½ ins.

Killed by Duke of Portland
27th Sep., 1919
Weight 17 st. 6 lbs.   Points 14
Width of Horn, inside 24 ins.
Thickness 4½ ins.

Illustrating Process of Growth of Antlers shed annually from 1911 to 1918 by stag killed that year by another stag.

Width of Horn, inside 34⅜ ins.   Thickness 4¾ ins.

antlers are just horns with tines or branches outcropping. This is entirely wrong. Antlers are made of a bony substance and obtain their nutriment from the outside, whilst the reverse is the case with horns. The skin covering of the antler during its growth or " velvet " period is saturated with blood and mucous drawn from the head and body of the stag, and the antler, being of bone construction and consequently porous, in turn absorbs the nutriment from the velvet, whereas horns of the bovine race have cores which feed them from the inside during the period of growth, and solidify as soon as the horns reach maturity. The horns of butting animals—goats, sheep, and antelope species—are hollow, and these animals use the front of the horns in attack.

Many explanations of the annual or periodical shedding of the antlers have been given, but none so far has been quite convincing. It has been taken for granted by several recent writers on this subject that deer owe their origin to Asia and migrated to Europe and other parts of the world from the East. This I think can only be accepted as an assumption, and we have just as much if not more evidence that they were denizens of the colder climes. To-day there are far more deer and more varieties beyond the sub-arctic line than below it, and the biggest species—caribou, elk (moose), and wapiti—are to-day parading in vast herds in the Northern parts of the American Continent, such as Newfoundland and Canada.

If it could be proved that deer are of cold clime origin the mystery of the shedding of the antlers might be less puzzling. When the ground is covered with snow, as it generally is in those parts for most of the year, the stag in order to find pasture scrapes away the snow, and the calf who is not strong enough to do this for himself is an interested looker-on until the patch is cleared. He then comes into action with his bullet head and butts his male parent out of the way, instinctively knowing that the head, and in fact the whole body of the stag is extremely sensitive during the period from the shedding of the antlers till the velvet disappears. The youngster then browses on the grass and by the time he is finished the stag has another clearance ready, and so on.   May it not be that the annual shedding of antlers is a provision of nature in the interests of his offspring and necessary to the continuance of the race ?

A UNIQUE HEAD.*

A three-antlered stag was shot by the Hon. George Monkton, afterwards Viscount Galway, in the Doon Burn, Langwell Forest, in 1873.

This stag had often been seen during the previous year at Langwell, by Donald Ross, head stalker, and was recognised by him, and also by his brother who was the stalker at Kinlochewe, Ross-shire, as the same beast at which Major Vaughan-Lee had fired fifteen shots in Dundonald Forest, Ross-shire, about 65 miles from Langwell.

The stag was also fired at in the Reay Forest.

Afterwards he came to Langwell, where he must have travelled about 80 miles before being killed by the Hon. George Monkton.

John Ross.

---

* I am indebted to His Grace the Duke of Portland for this information and for the unique photograph.

Three Antlered Stag

A Typical West Highland " Forest "

Ludovic MacLellan Mann, F.S.A., Scot.

The Deer in the Morning of the World

By LUDOVIC MACLELLAN MANN, F.S.A., Scot.

IN a survey of the history of the different families of deer one is constantly brought in contact with the episodes in which man has been associated with the animal in one way or another. His portrayal and his worship of the deer, his chasing, trapping and killing of it, and his utilisation of the different portions of its body, are all of considerable interest.

The circumstances of the discovery of ancient remains of the deer, antlers and bones, throw light on human history, while humanly-worked relics give us information as to the story of the deer. Neolithic or Late Stone Age Man, and man of the preceding Azilian period, if not also of even more remote periods, possessed certain domesticated animals, particularly the dog; but the waywardness of the deer family, with the exception of the sub-Arctic reindeer, prevented such close relationship. Neolithic converging earthen banks both in Belgium and Dumbartonshire, Scotland, are supposed to have been deer corrals and traps.

The earliest human remains found in Scotland are associated with utensils made from the antlers, chiefly of the red deer. Just as the various human and humanoid species gradually came upon the scene through the action of evolutionary processes and witnessed the dropping out of certain branches, so also was it with the deer family.

During practically the whole of the Great Cultural Period of some 100 millennia, when ancient man is known to have been at work in the European area, he encountered eight kinds of deer,

D

viz :—Cervus rangifer tarandus, the reindeer, *cervus sedgwicki, cervus maral,* the Siberian deer; *cervus megaceros hibernicus* or *cervus giganteus,* the Irish elk; *cervus elaphus,* the red deer; *cervus dama,* the fallow deer; *cervus capreolus* or *capreolus caprea,* the roe-deer, and *cervus alces* or *alces latifrons* or *alces machlis,* the moose.

During still earlier times other species of deer roamed over Europe. These animals of the Pliocene period, like the more modern deer, favoured different kinds of climate and moved to and fro across the Continent according to the fluctuations of climate. Among these very early deer were —*Cervus etenoides, cervus douvilii, cervus pardinensis, cervus carnutorum, cervus etueriarium* and *capreolus cusanus.* Contemporary with these forms were some of the still surviving deer. The moose at this remote time seems to have come into Europe. It is not yet understood in what part of the world these animals evolved to their present-day aspect. Considerable differences in the distribution of land and sea, compared with the modern geographical aspect, make the elucidation of this problem somewhat difficult.

When one considers the large number of species of deer at one time to be seen in Europe which have now become extinct or exceedingly scarce, one cannot but admire the capacity to survive inherent in the constitution of the reindeer, the roe-deer and the red deer, which have lived continuously in Europe from Pliocene times onwards.

Perhaps the most notable British deer which has everywhere become extinct was the Irish elk. Other deers which used to roam in the British area are now found in quite different regions; as for example, the reindeer, which survived in Britain in its more northern parts, such as in Sutherland and Caithness, until the end of the prehistoric period, about the beginning of this era. Its horns, sawn and cut by human hands, have been found in association with numerous relics deposited by man. While the reindeer survived in Scotland until quite late times chiefly in the most northern portions, it extended down into Ayrshire until the eve of the Roman occupation, if we are right in considering as genuine and authentic the humanly cut reindeer horns which were found a few years ago in the Lochlee Crannog (or marsh dwelling) in Ayrshire, Scotland.

Remains of the reindeer have also been found on the Clyde and other places in Scotland in pre-glacial and interglacial deposits. Its horns have been found on an ancient surface with remains of the mammoth at Kilmaurs, Ayrshire.

The reindeer entered the British area while there was still a land bridge to the Continent. As the climate fluctuated from epoch to epoch the reindeer moved north and south accordingly. Its most southern limits in Europe were Mentone and Northern Spain whither it penetrated apparently for the last time during one of the very cold periods, the Buehl, about 26,000 years before Christ.

The immediately following warm period saw the reindeer much farther north; but in the succeeding bad weather period the reindeer again predominated in Central Europe, about 17,000 B.C. Since that time this animal has been confined to the farthest north portions of Europe, and its place has been taken in Central Europe and Britain by the red deer.

Prehistoric archaeology, hand in hand with natural history and geology, tells of a succession of intrusions of the cold-loving reindeer towards southern parts and the pushing farther south of the warmth-loving red deer; with a reversal of the migrations during periods of more genial climatic conditions. The orderly succession of glacial or cold periods and mild or inter-glacial periods in Europe witnessed changes in flora and fauna, and indeed of the human occupation. The migrations were very slow, thousands of years intervening between one cold period and another.

Prehistoric man, as well as utilising the hide and tendons and eating the flesh of this deer, employed the antlers for a great variety of purposes. Palæolithic man loved to depict the figure of the deer on pieces of bone and stone, and to carve pictures of it in the round. This he did with surprising skill and artistic feeling, the drawings being exceedingly graphic and vivacious.

The discoveries of limestone caverns in Spain and France have disclosed incised and painted upon the walls portrayals of various animals, among which the reindeer and the red deer are prominent features. In some cases deer are shown grouped within the same panel. One of the most beautiful of these pictures, a polychrome painting on the wall of the cavern of De-Font-de-Gaume, Dordogne, shows two reindeer, one with palmated antlers, lying almost prostrate while another, a younger animal, its antlers larger but non-palmated, is looking at it as if in sympathy. It has recently been shown that this group as well as being of mythological value is in some fashion specially related to the planet Saturn, which among various ancient peoples symbolised death.

An examination of ancient barbed harpoon-heads shows the favourite material was either reindeer horn or the horn of the red deer. In the earlier period in Europe the harpoon-head of the reindeer horn predominated owing to the greater number of these animals in Western Europe at that time compared with other species of deer. At a later time when the climate improved and the red stag predominated the harpoon-heads were made of his horns. Owing to the difference in the texture of antler material it is found that the reindeer harpoons were round, while the later stag harpoons were flattish.

The industry of utilising antlers increased in importance as time went on. During the Azilian period a large number of fine handsome tools were made of the thicker portions of the red deer antler, which was sliced obliquely at one end and employed held in the hand as a smoother in the preparation of hides.

This class of object is among the relics of the earliest known humanly inhabited sites in Scotland.   The finest specimen of these yet noted I recently dug up on the Island of Risga, Loch Sunart.

During the Azilian and later times blocks of antler centrally perforated were used as heads of hammers, the shafts being probably made of wood.

In the shaft-mining of chalk (for flints to be made into tools) in the east of England about 9000 B.C., that is, mid-Neolithic times, the antlers of red deer were used as picks, and this tool was very generally used from that time onwards until the introduction and common use of metals.

At the end of the British Bronze Age, about 500 years B.C., and during the centuries immediately preceding and following the opening of the present era, there were all sorts of useful things fashioned out of antlers.   Perforated tines seem to have been used as cheek-pieces for horses' bridle bits and as handles of tools such as knives ; also pointed and socketed implements—some of them perhaps used as goads.

The gigantic Irish elk was perhaps the most interesting species of European deer.   It survived, though very sparingly, until about a century or two after the Roman intrusion into Britain.   The spread of its horns was enormous, measuring occasionally 13 feet across from tip to tip.   In later times it must have been more common in Ireland than in Britain ; but the increasing dampness of the Irish climate (which in recent epochs reached its maximum about the first century B.C.) and the consequent spread of bog and peat at the expense of the trees, seems to have told heavily against this deer in Ireland, whence it could not migrate.

The elk had very superior hardiness and staying power ; but in respect of adaptability and agility it must have been handicapped by the great size of its antlers.

In a small bog in the valley of Ballybatagh no fewer than 100 heads of elk have been discovered during the last half century.

Another huge member of the deer family, a Giant Stag, roamed over Western Europe during the extremely remote Chellean period about 56,000 years ago.

All the chronological estimates given in this note have been calculated by the author on a new system involving several independent and confirmatory lines of evidence.

Another deer of some importance to prehistoric man was the elk which inhabited the northern regions. Like the other species it moved backwards and forwards across the Continents according to climatic conditions. It was forest-loving. When the climate did not admit of forest growth this deer went elsewhere. It became practically extinct in Western Europe in Roman times. It roamed over the whole of the British area, and when Ireland and the Isle of Man emerged from the sea and Britain was cut off from the Continent, the elk remained in these islands, where its bones and horns have been found.

Its remains have been found in the late Pliocene or early Pleistocene land surfaces at Cromer in Norfolk.

Ludovic McL. Mann

Alex. Patience, F.S.A., Scot.

Ancient Deerstalkers, and Other Notes

By ALEXANDER PATIENCE, F.S.A., Scot.

Ancient Artists and Hunters.

DURING the past half century or more, there have been discovered in the Dordogne district in France, on the northern flank of the Pyrenees, and over a wide area in Spain, many caves and rock-shelters which have been the abode of Prehistoric Man. But it is only in comparatively recent years that the wonderful secrets of these caves have been given up to archæological research and have revealed to us a phase in the life of our ancestors so remarkable that for a long time it was regarded with incredulity.

For the most part these caverns—many of them extending for considerable distances into the heart of the hills—have, in the course of geologic time, been formed in limestone rock by water percolating from above and dissolving out the calcareous material. The comfort they offered was eagerly embraced by the Ancient Hunter in the severe climatic conditions which obtained in the Aurignacian, and which became much intensified in the Magdalenian stage of the Upper Palæolithic era.

In common with all hunting peoples the Aurignacian had abundant leisure and he studied his physical surroundings to some purpose. He was living in the midst of a great Mammalian fauna, and in his constant struggle with the Cave-bear, the Cave-lion, the Rhinoceros and other carnivora which have now been long extinct another side of his character was awakened—the

artistic sense was developed—and he gradually learned to repro-
duce these animals in carving, in sculpture and in the polychrome
paintings which adorn the walls of so many of these caverns.
These works of Art, which probably reached their finest phase in
the Middle Magdalenian period, were executed with so much
marvellous delicacy and realism that, when the attention of the
world was drawn to them, their high antiquity was for long
regarded with scepticism.

The first scientists who shed light upon this wonderful phase of
human culture were the great archæologists, Edouard Lartet, a
Frenchman and H. Christy, an Englishman,*by their painstaking
researches in the caves and rock-shelters of Dordogne.

THE EARLIEST PICTURE IN THE WORLD.

The stations of this Province have probably yielded the greatest
treasures, in these memorials of Primitive Man, but our interest, as
deer-stalkers at least, is transferred to the Grotto of Lorthet, in
the High Pyrenees, where the eminent French Archæologist,
Edouard Piette, discovered a reindeer antler upon which the
figures of *three red deer* were carved by one of our ancestors
thousands of years before a stone of the great Egyptian Pyramids
was laid.

As will be seen from Piette's reproduction,†part of the engraving
has, unfortunately, been effaced, but what remains has shown that
the Palæolithic artist had depicted with great fidelity the form of
dead deer.‡ The work is undoubtedly a wonderful picture of still

---

* " Reliquiæ Acquitanicæ," 1875.

† " L'Art pendant l'age du Renne," Pls. 39-40.

‡ Some controversy took place a few years ago as to the original lines of the effaced
part of this carving. Sir Ray Lankester essayed two restorations—the first being
known to me through Parkyn's " Prehistoric Art," and the second from Lankester's
" Secrets of Earth and Sea," the latter being executed under the direction of Mr
Walter Winans. Both these authors believe that the picture represents *deer in motion,*
but it appears to me they are in error. I cordially agree with Mr Allan Gordon

Red Deer and Salmon incised on a piece of reindeer antler, from Lorthet,
High Pyrenees. (After Piette).

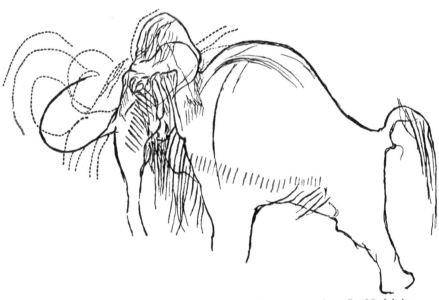

Charging Mammoth engraved on a piece of ivory tusk, from La Madelaine.
(After E. Lartet)·

The running Reindeer, engraved on hornblende schist, from Saint Marcel. (After Breuil).

Photo by Whyte & Sons, Glasgow

8-point Antler, abnormal type (brow, bay and tray, and unforked top). From Ardgoil.

life, and the artist in order to show all the grace and beauty of the head of his 16-pointer had drawn it round in the posture seen in the carving. Sir Ray Lankester has pointed out that, in the sense of it being a composition, it is " the earliest picture in the world " and its great artistic merit and high antiquity should irresistibly appeal to the heart of every ardent stalker. That our artist, however, could depict the most spirited action is well seen in such charming pictures as the Charging Mammoth (La Madeleine) and the Galloping Reindeer (Saint Marcel), engraved as Breuil points out " avec un vigueur et une sureté de main incomparable."

Not here, indeed, the crude effort of a degenerate savage, nor the distorted shapes of anarchic present-day " Expressionism," but artistic productions which, as Professor Boule says, " bear striking evidence of real aesthetic sense, a masterly realism, skilled technique, and great strength of execution . . . . master-pieces of life and movement."* Or if we regard the group of polychrome figures on the roof of the celebrated cavern of Alta-mira we may see with Breuil and Cartailhac works of Art which place the old artists of the glyptic age far above the animal painters of Greece and all the classical civilisations of the East. So, from those bone engravings and mural paintings found in the caves and grottos of Lorthet, Altamira, Font de Gaume and others, we obtain a vivid picture of what manner of man our Cromagnard stalker was.

Cameron, with whom I have discussed the matter, and who has thrown much light upon some obscure points, that "the Palæolithic artist drew his picture from dead models and did not suppose them to be anything else." I was somewhat puzzled when first I read Winan's graphic account of the stag "moving in real action" and at the same time " taking a last look round before the herd goes out of sight," because I have watched hundreds of startled stags move swiftly away and know that they *always* stopped dead before glancing back to the rear.

From the number of points seen in the engraving the middle stag is either a 12- or 14-pointer ; the latter, if bay tines are present. In the first restoration he is graciously invested with the insignia of royalty, but in the second Winans has administered the " unkindest cut of all " by dethroning him from the purple.

* Marcellin Boule, " Fossil Men," p. 257.

E

THE SOUL OF THE ANCIENT HUNTER.

Life must have been anything but a bed of roses for the ancient hunter. Nature had not endowed him with many material comforts ; pottery was then unknown; he had no domesticated animals, and the art of agriculture was still in the dim and distant future. But the bones of the cave-bear, rhinoceros, bison and mammoth, found in abundance among the debris of the caves, bear eloquent testimony to the unflinching courage with which he held his own in the grim struggle for existence which obtained in these far-off days.

Yet withal, as Boule rightly points out, he was " peaceful and gentle in character " and all the memorials which Prehistoric Man has left behind him during the greater part at least of the Palæolithic Age show what his main pre-occupations have been.*

And, again, we see, in his sculptures representing funeral rites and worship of the dead, evidence of that great mysterious urge which lifted his mind beyond his merely physical surroundings to ponder on the unseen. Think of him for a moment—the day's hunting done, lying on his rugged bed under a starlit sky, the ghostly forms of wild carnivora for ever lurking around him in the gloom, and amidst those perils, drawing aside half-fearfully in his mind's eye the curtain of that mysterious shadowy land which nightly he encounters in his dreams, and eagerly straining to understand its riddle—and we have the picture of a man of high fortitude and courage and of great mental and moral qualities.

It may be, and probably is, true that these paintings and sculptures had some relation to the hunter's magical rites. The animals represented were of two kinds, those he hunted for food and the great carnivora, and his aim probably was on

---

* For the innate peacefulness of the Primitive Hunter, see W J. Perry, in " War and Civilisation," Bull, of the John Rylands Library, 1918. For the origin and development of organised warfare, see the same author's works, " The Children of the Sun," London, 1923 ; and " The Growth of Civilisation," London, 1924.

the one hand to facilitate capture and on the other to win protection.

The meaning and scope of this sympathetic magic have recently been fully and very ably discussed by Perry* and Professor G. E. Smith,† but it is difficult to believe that this practice alone inspired those hunters to such great artistic heights. Rather does it seem that their art was in essence the outcome of that spirit of imitation which is inherent in man, and slowly developing from crude beginnings blossomed in the Magdalenian age into the fairest flower of Prehistoric Art.

Since the day the Palæolithic artist and hunter left his enduring memorial on the Lorthet Antler, mankind has plodded over a long and weary trail—a trail strewn with the wrecks of mighty civilisations. And it may be refreshing, when every horizon to-day is darkened with social and political storm-clouds, to live again for a little while with these valiant hunters, with the men who hunted the wolf, the boar and the cave-lion and who stalked the mammoth, the bison and the wild stag.

The Evolution of the Antler.

The beautifully branched antler which we have seen in the stag of the Lorthet engraving is comparatively speaking the product of recent geological times. Going gradually back from the Pleistocene age we find the antler becoming more and more simple and unbranched, until in the older Oligocene beds of France the primitive ancestors of the deer are entirely destitute of these appendages but are provided with long canine tusks which would be quite formidable organs of offence and defence.

This last stage is represented to-day by the Chinese water-deer (*Hydrelaphus inermis*) which is found among the reeds and long

---

* " The Origin of Magic and Religion," London, 1923.
† " The Evolution of the Dragon," Manchester, 1919.

grass on the banks and islands of the Yang-tsi-Kiang, and which is
quite a pygmy, standing only 20 inches high at the withers. It is
devoid of antlers, but the male is armed with long curved canine
teeth—those of the female being smaller. It probably represents
a very ancient type of the deer family, although as Lydekker tells
us, no fossils so far have been referred to it.

The Upper Oligocene beds of St. Gerand-le-Puy, France, have
yielded the remains of a hornless cervuline genus known as
Dremotherium. The scenery and fauna of this ancient Allier
basin must then have been vastly different from its appearance
to-day. We can picture great swamps surrounding small and
shallow lakes denizened by turtles and crocodiles, pelicans, ibis
and flamingos, and probably in the neighbouring forests were to be
found monkeys and lemurs. Frequenting these swamps were
herds of the antlerless *Dremotherium*, and in this genus Lydekker
sees the ancestral type of the modern Old World Deer.*

In the succeeding Miocene, the Golden Age of Mammals—the
hornless race has now passed away in Europe—we come on
antlers upon long pedicles from which they are imperfectly
differentiated by a burr.

Adolf Rörig† has made an exhaustive study of these fossil
antlers and has described and figured many specimens. He has
made an attempt to straighten out the mixed synonymy of these
ancient cervine genera, but it is a difficult task, for as Hans
Gadow‡ has observed " Finality is impossible until we know for
certain whether the separately found pedicles and antlers, or both
together, are successive stages of one species, or represent the
armaments of several adult species, or genera, which did not pass
beyond the respective stages of broachers, forkers, etc."

In brief, " the earliest antler in the historical evolution of the

* " Deer of All Lands," p. 216.
† Archiv. für Entwick. der Organ., Leipzig, 1900, 10, pp. 525/617. Pls. v.-xii.
‡ " The Evolution of Horns and Antlers "—Proc. Zool. Soc., Mar. 1902, p. 217.

stag carries the brow tine on an unbranched beam (Miocene) ; next comes the tray tine along with the forked top (Pliocene) ; and lastly, the bay tine (Pleistocene) which completes the summing of a typical stag."[*]

Thus the steps taken in the development of the antler in the stag to-day is a recapitulation of the general outlines of its evolutionary history.

But it sometimes looks as if Nature took a keen delight in disturbing the tranquillity of the Naturalist by springing upon him problems which he often finds difficult to understand. We have reproduced the photograph of the antlers of an 8-pointer stag, one of a band of four which fell to my rifle on the Ardgoil hill-tops in October, 1921. We have here antlers with brow, *bay* and tray tines, but with *un*forked tops. It is impossible at present to say whether the forked top has definitely dropped out in the antler development in this case, or whether it would develope out of its normal order in the year *after* the appearance of the bay tine. The former would seem more likely. This shows a departure from the view expressed above where the forked top is developed *prior* to the birth of the bay tine. This is the only specimen of this type of antler which I have met in the field, having examined approximately three hundred heads during the past seven or eight years, although on the other hand the frequency with which I came across regressive and decadent heads, especially the latter, was disconcerting.

With a view to seeing how far this type of antler prevailed I approached recently several leading taxidermists who have handled many scores of antlers. The subject, however, has apparently not so far received much scientific consideration, but Mr Charles Kirk, of Glasgow, has been good enough to look over his old stock of antlers and has shown me two pairs and a right

---

* Allan Gordon Cameron—" The Wild Red Deer of Scotland," 1923, p. 129.

'cast' belonging to this type, the one shown in illustration being a particularly graceful specimen. The stag was shot in Fearnan Forest in October, 1914.

Mr Kirk appears to think that this type of antler is uncommon.

Mr Macleay, Taxidermist, Inverness, who has passed many thousands of antlers through his hands, informs me that he has seen quite a number of this type, and which is also interesting, antlers *with brows, bays, and no trays or forked tops.* He believes that the type in question although not rare, is nevertheless not very common.

We have, therefore, unfortunately, not sufficient data to enable us to form any safe estimate as to the frequency with which this type of antler occurs in relation to the normal, but it is probably very small.

There can, however, be little doubt, I think, as to the broad evolutionary path taken by the antler. In Pliocene times the 8-pointer (without bay tines) was common, and it was apparently not until the Pleistocene age that the stag assumed his badge of " royalty." In the devolution or degeneration of the stag's antlers—which may be due to various causes—the bay tines which were his latest acquisition are, as a rule, the first to disappear. The abnormal type of antler above described may be—not a further stage in the development of the antler—but a regression to an earlier type. If so, the regression has taken place by an unusual route, not involving the loss of the bay tine which was the *last* acquired, but cutting out the development of the forked tops, the *last but one* stage in ordinary development. The hereditary basis for this unusual form of development is quite unknown at present.

A PROBLEM IN NATURAL HISTORY.

As is well known a stag sheds its antlers annually, usually in April, and immediately thereafter new ones begin to grow, which are by the end of August or the beginning of September again in perfect fighting condition. But the solution of the problem as to the origin and use of the deciduous antler has proved to be as elusive as a will o' the wisp and has lured our naturalists into many a scientific bog.

One would naturally assume that the antler was designed as a weapon for use against other species, but it is a remarkable fact that the stag is dispossessed of his armament at a time when he is not physically fit to withstand the onslaught of his enemies, in the form of wolves and other carnivora, which are for ever dogging his heels.

Hunger and love are the two great dominating forces in the animal world, and the latter is probably the more powerful. In the season of courtship amongst all mammalian life fierce jealousies occur between rivals, and in all males endowed with special fighting weapons mortal conflicts very often ensue, and the possession of the desired mate or mates is decided by law of battle.

Darwin held the view that the deer's antlers were sexual weapons acquired for this purpose* but later admitted that a *single point* would be more dangerous than the *branched antler* and " the suspicion has therefore crossed my mind that they may serve in part as *ornaments*."†

That the antler cannot altogether have been acquired for the purpose of fighting his rival may be seen in the fact that " bald or hummel stags are frequently masters of large herds and hold their hinds against all comers."‡ The interesting point in the theory of Sexual Selection as to the choice made by the female through the display of the male's charms has no weight here, as the stag takes energetic measures with his harem and is ruthless,

---

* " Origin of Species," 6th ed., p. 64.
† " The Descent of Man," 2nd ed., p. 511.
‡ Cameron, op. cit., p. 124

insisting on his mating rights. Professor J. T. Cunningham* and Dr Gadow have very fully and ably discussed the use and evolution of the deciduous antler and the latter comes to the conclusion that their possession " amounts to an enormous waste of energy and material during the life of the owner " and " although full of grace and beauty " are " morphologically very faulty structures, as wastefully contrived as the shedding of the thousands of teeth of Sharks and Crocodiles."†

THE COMING OF THE WILD STAG.

It is now pretty well agreed among palæontologists that the primeval home of the *Cervus elaphus* group lay in Central Asia, probably somewhere between the Altai and the Tian-Shan Mountains, or upon the Pamir Watershed. One stream of migrants, moving out in the wake of the setting sun found their path " marked out for them by geographical conditions . . . . North of the Caucasus Mountains, all routes from Asia to Europe were barred by an immense sheet of water, the Aralo-Caspian of geology, which, uniting the Black Sea, the Caspian, and the Sea of Aral, flooded the South Russian and Siberian Steppes, and, finding no outlet at the Bosphorus, discharged northwards, probably into the Gulf of Obb. South of the Caucasus, on the other hand, and rising abruptly along the southern shores of the Aralo-Caspian Sea, successive mountain ranges extended without a break from the Hindu-Kush through North Persia to the Caucasus, and from the Caucasus through Asia Minor to the Balkans, finally merging in the vast amphitheatre of forest-clad heights—Alps and Carpathians—which embosom the " tiefland " of Hungary. By this direct and obvious path ancestral red deer travelled to Central Europe from Central Asia and could not have travelled otherwise."‡

---

* " Sexual Dimorphism in the Animal Kingdom," 1900, pp. 73-9.
† Gadow op., cit., pp. 217-218.
‡ Cameron, op., cit., p. 236.

Photo by Whyte & Sons, Glasgow

8-point Antler, abnormal type, Fearnan Forest.

8-point Antler, abnormal type. Forest unknown. Specimen depressed towards camera to show the form of the "double brows."

Stag, painted in red, from La Pasiega, Upper Aurignacian (after Breuil).

Cameron has given in his classical work an interesting map showing the European centre of dispersion and the probable routes taken by the stag in his migration westward until he reached the far flung outposts of the British Isles.

But part of this stream had hived off, taking a south-westerly route probably through Greece and Sicily, reaching the North African shore by way of the Italian landbridge and now represented by the so-called Barbary Deer of Algiers and Morocco.

It is known that the early Pleistocene was a period of considerable continental elevation ; Great Britain and Ireland were joined to the Continent, Corsica and Sardinia to Italy, and the land-bridges to Africa and Sicily were the routes by which the intercourse of Mammalian life took place.

This North African race—which is apparently confined to Tunisia and Algeria, and which, with the wonderful adaptability of the wild red deer to changing environment is found roaming the treeless plains around Douirat—is smaller than the typical and generally wants the bay tines which may be due as Lydekker suggests to degeneracy in consequence of an environment not so well suited to full development as in northern climes.

The wild red deer is still widely distributed in the temperate regions of Europe and Asia, but in many parts of Europe, where at one time it roamed in all its pristine splendour, it is now represented only by its fossilised bones. The stag of the old Cromagnard artist may still be seen, occasionally, in the virgin forests of the Caucasus, Asia Minor and the Carpathians, where civilisation has not yet laid its ruthless hand.

The members of our own hardy island race are dwarfed and stunted in comparison with these Monarchs of the Forest, hemmed up as they are within the narrow confines of our sea-girt isle, ekeing out a scanty subsistence for the most part on bare hillsides and wind-swept glens, and severed for centuries from ancestral stock. The wild stag of our highland hills, although

F

not comparable in weight of body, nor in spread of antler, to his Pleistocene ancestor, is yet in his grace of outline and majestic bearing a Thing of Beauty and for ever a joy to the hunter. What he has lost in weight he has probably gained in mental fibre, and he may be more the master of his Fate.

For Nature

> " Winnows, winnows roughly, sifts,
>   To dip her chosen in her source.
>   Contention is the vital force
>   Whence pluck they brain, her prize of gifts."

The frugal fare and rigorous climatic environment have doubtless immensely sharpened his wits and endowed him with greater grit, just as they have helped to mould the Highlander who has hunted him for hundreds of years into one of the finest and hardiest races in the world.

That the stag can give the stalker an occasional thrill—a thrill which he expects to encounter only in an African Forest or an Indian Jungle—the passing of a noble 10-pointer will show.

An Episode of the Hills.

The game of stalking the wild stag on the high hills is usually a battle of wits against wits, and occasionally there are risks to stalker and stalked, the odds, however, being about a thousand to one against the—stalked.

One day in October, 1923, in company with a gallant Highlander Stalker Robert Cameron, I had been following the " spoor " along a steep slope close to the ridge of one of the low-lying hills in Ardkinglas on the western side of Loch Fyne, from the top of which a splendid view of Glenshira is obtained a mile or so beyond.

Cautiously rounding a boulder I espied my quarry about 200 yards ahead.   He had apparently been moving along in front but had stopped, his head turned round towards us—a characteristic pose. We were stalking upwind but a slight displacement of debris on our part had flashed a warning signal to his active brain and he was on the alert and had started to go.   In a moment my Lee-Enfield had spat out its swift little courier of death, but almost simultaneously with the rifle's crack the stag swung uphill at the trot and disappeared over a ridge.

Surely not a miss !   Or had I only grazed his wither ?   For a deer which has been vitally wounded about the heart or lungs, if it does not instantly fall, usually bounds away at the gallop and downhill.   I hastened forward along my line of fire, Cameron following about three paces behind.   We had traversed about 150 yards when I suddenly caught sight of the stag's surroyals on the skyline about 50 feet above.   At that moment a swirl of the breeze blew uphill over us and on to the stag, which instantly got our " wind."   Coming slowly to the edge of the ridge, he poised himself for about three seconds and then bore down upon us like a bolt from a catapult.   Cameron shouted a warning but I had already instinctively " ducked " although there was not a blade of grass under which to take cover.   He flashed past between us with the rush of a whirlwind, shot down some 150 feet and rolled over—dead.   Phew !

In extremis my antagonist was magnificent.   Although only a fleeting glance, I can still picture his splendid pose, his flashing eye, and his head erect and defiant.   If, instead of a " miss " he had scored a " bull " in his last desperate charge could either of us have bemoaned our fate ?   As I gazed on his graceful form, lying stretched on the heather, his eyes now partially glazed in death, I could only answer in the negative.   What's sauce for the goose ! An examination showed that he had been vitally shot—my bullet had grazed his lungs.   He was a 10-pointer, but without bay-tines—a decadent—a " throw back."   He died, however, as game as any of the proud and imperial race from which he sprung —his face to the foe.

THE LURE OF THE HIGHLAND HILLS.

To those who are sound in wind and limb there is nothing more stimulating to mind and body than ranging over a Highland Hill. Far up in the heights of Ardgoil with the open vault of heaven above and at our feet the rolling sweep of knoll and glen and hill-top, and with no discordant civilised note breaking into the solitude, we have the feeling of absolute freedom and a sense of the open spaces.

In this domain the discerning ear and eye can learn much of Wild Nature's story, especially if the Naturalist be blended with the Sportsman. Our interest need never flag for we can watch the hill fauna at play, at courtship, or in the more deadly occupation of securing a meal.

We may have flushed a covey and witnessed the flight of the rare and beautiful Ptarmigan, or have followed the majestic sweep of the Golden Eagle overhead, or, more alluring, we may catch a fleeting glimpse of the Peregrine as, dropping like a bolt from the blue, it strikes with unerring aim a flying grouse, or in the stillness of an autumn evening we may hear the distant scream of a mountain hare, that tells of an ever-recurring drama of the hills. Although it is not possible to read the full story of wild mountain life—even could we understand all we see—for the black pall of night hides much from our ken, yet to study it in most of its moods and to get in closer touch with the lives of its denizens, we must breast these hills in all seasons and in all weathers, not only under the blue of a summer sky, or when the autumnal hillside is a mosaic of green and purple and gold, but also when the hilltops are one unbroken undulating sheet of glistening white; when the sound of Heaven's Artillery is reverberating with deafening roar from ravine to hill-top and from hill-top to ravine ; when the hail bites savagely into our cheeks ; when the blizzard is raking mountain peak and glen and the storm clouds, like the Valkyries, go scudding across the sky. And to stalk the wild stag under these conditions, even without the consummation of the "kill," brings a joy indescribable.   We are for a brief period under the grip of the primitive.

Yesterday and To-Day

Hunter calls to hunter across the centuries and often as I lie on the hill-top, behind some rock or patch of heather watching the wild quarry, I see in imagination the Cromagnard stalker— just as he is pictured by the artist of Laugerie-Basse, crouching behind a bison with uplifted spear—gallantly risking life and limb upon the deftness of a spear-throw, and as my gaze wanders to my modern magazine rifle I ponder upon the difference between then and now.

Is it, after all, only a difference between spear and rifle, or of "toga and tunic"?   Across these intervening millennia what have we gained, not in material greatness nor in scientific attainment, but in moral fibre?   To-day, with a world in chaos, one wonders!   But we have faith that our race will yet emerge from the shadows rejuvenated, triumphant, strong, and like the return of Persephone from the Underworld will be

> " . . . a mighty joy
> To gods and mortal men."

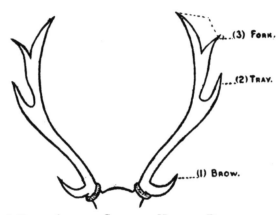

(3) Fork.

(2) Tray.

(1) Brow.

8 Point Antler, Showing Normal Development.

With Sketchbook and With Rifle

By V. R. BALFOUR-BROWNE, B.A. (Oxford).

HAVE stalked Red-deer in Scotland in most of the months of the year, armed with glass, sketchbook and pencil in the majority of those months, and in the all too short stalking season with rifle as well.

There is a great fascination in stalking without a rifle, for as someone said, one of the chief attractions of stalking is that it takes you to places that you would certainly never visit for any other purpose.

But it must be confessed that the pleasure of outwitting a deer, for the sake of making a drawing of him, is but very small beer compared with the joy of outwitting a deer because one wants to kill him. In truth the enjoyment of the former is due to a large extent to the fact that, to use Mr Jorrocks' phrase with a slightly different meaning, it is " the image of war without the guilt." One likes to make a success of the stalk in July, because it is just what may happen in September ; and if one does succeed in getting comfortably " in " at a good stag in velvet, one enjoys the feeling that, were it only two months later, one would have him dead all right—if only he would turn broadside !

It must be confessed also that although one likes to succeed in the off-season stalks, the trouble, inconvenience, and discomfort necessary to success are always a consideration in the choice of what to stalk. In September, trouble, inconvenience and discomfort simply do not count—they are all in the day's work—

and nothing matters if you get him.   But in July—well that ugly brute down on the flat is certainly not so good a beast as that one up there below the top ; but—it's a long climb round to the top— the day is hot, and any way that ugly brute may be just as good to make a drawing of—so one just crawls down the burn !

This confession may shock some people.   I have heard it said that the stalking part of the business is great fun, but as for shooting the beast—" one might just as well shoot a donkey ! "   I am sorry, but I must confess that I entirely disagree.

In *The Field* of June 12th, 1924, there appeared an article under the title " The Meaning of Sport."   The writer, who signed himself " ·256 " had been out for two days after a particular black buck with a particularly good head.   Having fresh-found him on the third day, he spent hours in trying to drive him on to ground where a stalk would be possible.   At last, after many futile attempts, the buck appearing to enter into the spirit of the game, ·256 crawled over a ridge and found his quarry within twenty yards of him—and then—" The rest was butchery.   I had come over the ridge on my belly and looked at him through a bush.   I had only to raise the rifle and he was done, when a revulsion of feeling came over me.   Why should I kill him ?   I had won, won hands down, and I would exercise my prerogative of mercy, so I stood up and took my hat off to him."

Now, that I fully understand, and I take off my hat to ·256. But ·256 would, I feel sure, agree that the thing would have had no piquancy, would in fact simply not have occurred at all, unless he had been out with intent to kill.   It was, I suggest, that desire to kill, strange and primitive perhaps, that gave zest to the whole pursuit.   It was that which made the expenditure of so much energy worth while, and it was that which made the exercise of the prerogative of mercy worth while also.

There is, nevertheless, as has been said, a great fascination about what may be called " glass and sketch-book " stalking, and this is partly due to the fact that one does *see* more than when one is out with intent to kill.

Mr William Long propounds a theory in his delightful book "How Animals Talk," to the effect that wild creatures are able to perceive the "intention" with which man tries to approach them. "As you go quietly through the woods, projecting your own 'aura' of peace or sympathy, it may be, in an invisible wave ahead of you, there is nothing disturbing or inharmonious in either your thoughts or your actions ; and at times the wild animal seems curiously able to understand the one as well as the other, just as certain dogs know at first glance whether a stranger is friendly or hostile, or afraid of them. When you are excited or lustful to kill, something of your emotional excitement seems to precede you ; it passes over many wild birds and beasts, all delicately sensitive, before you come within their sense range ; and when you draw near enough to see them you often find them restless, suspicious, though as yet no tangible warning of danger has floated through the still woods." Personally, I am afraid I am very doubtful of this theory, but whether there is truth in it or not, the unarmed stalker certainly does see more—possibly merely because this is what he is out for, namely to see !

He may waste many a day in this occupation without seeing anything of particular interest, but he will occasionally be rewarded by the sight of something beautiful, something tragic, or something humorous, which he might never have had time to see, had he been intent upon circumventing one particular stag.

I remember once wasting an August afternoon watching and sketching a little group of hinds that were feeding and snoozing in the sunshine. After some time I noticed an old hind wander off to a peat hag, where she proceeded to wallow. On the far bank of the hag stood a young hind with her head on one side watching the antics of the old lady in her bath, and quite obviously making facetious remarks ! There really was no doubt about it

G

—one could almost hear them from the expression on the creature's face ; and obviously too the old lady resented them, for she suddenly jumped out of her bath and let out viciously with her hind legs at the impertinent flapper ! The latter, however, apparently expected some such sign of resentment, for she avoded the flying heels with a neat side step, and cantered gaily away !

Although in the above anecdote impertinence and resentment have been attributed to the two hinds, it is never really safe to judge the actions of wild animals according to human standards.

From time to time one hears, and I myself have occasionally seen, instances of what is called sympathy or friendship, or perhaps instances of extraordinary intelligence on the part of wild deer.

It is, however, very doubtful whether these words, in their ordinary sense as applicable to human emotions, are applicable to the mental processes of wild deer at all. One is apt to forget that in all probability the paramount instinct in the minds of wild animals is that of self-preservation, tempered only by an instinct for the preservation of the race. The maternal instinct, which appears to contradict the instinct for self-preservation, is after all only an instance of the main instinct for self being subservient to that for the benefit of the race.

The more one observes deer in the wild state, the more one will be struck by the apparent intelligence of their actions on some occasions, and the apparent imbecility of their actions on others. In other words, one will become more and more convinced that one cannot judge of their mental processes according to human standards at all.

Anyone who has engaged in stalking will doubtless remember instances similar to those I am about to relate.

I had stalked down among the rocks to within fifty yards of a knobber and a three-year-old stag that were quietly feeding. The former suddenly looked up and saw my head move as I sketched him. My cap was a good colour, and very little of my face showed above the rock, and from the moment the knobber caught sight of me, I remained absolutely still. The little beast was, however, convinced that he had seen something. He stood at gaze for perhaps a minute, and then apparently wishing his companion, who was still quietly feeding, to know of his suspicions, he trotted round close to his nose and again stood at gaze. The three-year-old raised his head, looked round, but seeing nothing returned to his grazing. My knobber friend repeated his manœuvre and again stood at gaze. This time the other took no notice at all. This indifference exasperated the suspicious knobber. He turned on his friend, stood up on his hind legs, and gave him two sharp raps on the shoulder with his forefeet— standing at gaze in my direction once more, as soon as his feet touched earth again.

This appeared to convince the three-year-old that there must be something to account for the other's nervousness. He now had a good look round, and although he still saw nothing to cause alarm, consented to follow his companion over the ridge and round the corner—out of my sight.

Once, just after the stalking season was over, I stalked a nice Royal, who was ramping and roaring round his twenty or thirty hinds. I got to within about a hundred yards of him, and having a comfortable place behind a big block of granite, settled down to my work. Just after I had done so, he got tired of rampaging about, and wandered quietly away from his hinds—straight towards me. When he came within five yards of my block of granite I sat up and showed myself. I confess I had no fancy to be within range of his antlers when he first saw me. With a snort of astonished fear he galloped *ventre a terre* back towards the hinds. The hinds recognised alarm in his gallop, and "bunched" preparatory to flight. But at that moment there came a challenging roar from another stag, somewhere down on the flats behind me. Whereupon the Royal completely forgot me! He answered the rival on the flats, rounded up his hinds, and drove them back in my direction ; he then began rampaging about as before, and for the next quarter of an hour was never more than 120 yards from me, and often within 60.

Now the knobber showed, one must admit, what appeared to be considerable intelligence.   But what is to be said of the Royal ?

It is true that domestic worries are apt to affect the intelligence even of human beings ; and this Royal stag had, it was clear, much to worry him.   But can one imagine an animal to have even a spark of human intelligence, when, having just seen one of his hereditary enemies hiding behind a rock, he takes no further notice of that enemy because, forsooth, another animal of his own kind threatens to take away one of his twenty or thirty wives ?   Even the instinct for self-preservation would seem in this instance to have given way to mere stupidity !

But it may be said, if the hereditary enemy had been armed with something more dangerous than a sketch-book, the Royal would not have ignored him as he did.

Here is another instance, then.   The enemy on this occasion was armed with a rifle, and the stag had not the excuse of domestic worries for his stupidity.

We had succeeded in getting within a hundred yards of a fair eleven pointer that was lying down all alone at the foot of a big rock.   My friend, for whom I was acting as ghillie, was comfortably " positioned " behind a heathery bank, with the rifle ready.   As the stag lay with his stern towards us, a lying shot was out of the question.   I therefore left my friend, crawled back and round to a knoll some fifty yards to his right, and " showed a handkerchief." The stag did exactly what we hoped.   He rose and stared at me, offering a full broadside to my friend.   Click !—followed by the rattle of the magazine—the cartridge had missed fire !   That betrayed the presence of a second hereditary enemy, and the

A Nice Royal

stag transferred his gaze from me to my friend—but he didn't move ! The next cartridge in the clip functioned all right, and

> At the shot the forest denizen
> Lay dead as mutton, in fact was venison;

and serve him right !

Another stag, I remember, was missed at seventy yards, hit low at a hundred yards, and killed at a hundred and thirty yards. And for each shot he stood broadside on, gazing at his executioner !

One would have expected the second to have been sufficient warning as to the unhealthiness of that particular corrie. But the facts were as stated. I should add, moreover, that the second shot would not have interfered with his powers of running away ; it only inflicted a flesh wound from which he might very likely have recovered.

Another factor which contributes to the pleasure of stalking merely " to see," is the fact that one is generally " on one's own." You have to find out for yourself whether there is sufficient cover to hide you as you crawl down the burn ; you have to guess how the wind will be blowing when you reach the burn. These things are often *known* by the professional stalker who is leading you in an actual stalk, and a large part of the interest of the stalk may therefore be denied you.

This in fact is the chief complaint of some people, who decry the sport of deerstalking as practised in Scotland to-day. The stalker, they say, has all the fun ; the " gentleman " merely shoots when he is told to. And there is a good deal in this complaint.

A strange fetish exists in connection with the sport, an idea that no one can even attempt to stalk a stag unless, as the phrase goes, " he knows the ground as he knows his own drawing room."

What would happen if he did make such an attempt is left to the imagination. The only result in actual fact would be, of course, that the amateur in all probability would be successful rather less often than the professional. Otherwise, provided he is willing to accept advice on such points as what ground should be left quiet in certain winds, and what is a shootable beast, no very dire consequences would follow the amateur's possibly ill-conceived and ill-executed, efforts.

What ground should be left quiet in certain winds is undoubtedly of considerable importance. On some forests an east wind has a curiously unsettling effect upon deer. I have seen long lines of deer marching eastwards, though quite undisturbed in the ordinary sense, simply because the wind had veered to the east, and a strange restlessness had taken possession of them in consequence. To have moved them under such circumstances, would certainly have driven large herds across the march, and might have injured the stalking on that particular forest for the rest of the season.

There is also more in the question of what is a shootable beast than some people imagine. It is easy enough to recognise as shootable a true " monarch of the glen," if one is lucky enough to see one. But to be sure that the best of a small herd with nothing outstanding in it is *good enough,* is by no means always easy. Perhaps he has been rolling in a peat hag, and looks much bigger than his clean companions. It is odd how *dirt* appears to increase the creature's proportions. His antlers, too, may look black and strong. It is worth remembering that a back view of a head, always appears to flatter its strength. If by chance, while one is considering the problem, a really shootable beast should appear, one may be astonished at the comparative insignificance of the peat-blackened fellow, and at having given him a second thought at all. Or again, perhaps you have found two or three in a herd about which you have no doubt. One of them you have set your heart on, having counted, shall we say, twelve points on his antlers, when spying them before " going in." You successfully reach the chosen firing point and push the rifle forward.   There they all are, a hundred yards below you, but they've got their heads up, something has disturbed them, and, to your ungrammatical consternation, you are not sure now " which is him " !

The experience of an old hand is invaluable on such occasions ; but if the amateur recognises his own shortcomings, and is willing to take advice, there is really no reason why he should not take an intelligent part in the sport, even to the extent of taking command and conducting the stalk himself, if he so desires.   To my mind there is no doubt about it, that to find, stalk, and kill a good stag *oneself* is the best and most satisfying achievement that any sport in this country can afford.

I find that I have only hinted at what is, perhaps, the greatest joy of all that is the accompaniment of stalking at any season of the year.   It is, to put it shortly, simply being on the hill.

To describe the effects of light and shade, of sunshine and shadow, mist and storm, amid the high hills is beyond the power of most pens, and it will not be here attempted.   But even when description is attempted with success, mere description gives but little idea of the spiritual uplift the sight of such things gives.

Seeing such things is part of the job of one who goes to the hill armed with a sketch book ; and one loves it.   Recording with a paint-brush what has been seen is another part of the job ; and one loves that too.

But alas !   So little of the love with which one *sees*, seems to be infused into the record upon paper !

V. R. Balfour-Browne

The Rt. Hon. Sir Herbert Maxwell, Bart., F.R.S.

The Red Deer of Galloway

By the Rt. Hon. Sir HERBERT MAXWELL, Bart.
F.R.S., D.C.L., LL.D.

A T the head of Wigtown Bay there lies a wide expanse of alluvium formed of detritus brought down from the Galloway upland by the rivers Cree and Bladenoch. The estuary of the Cree meanders through this plain for a distance of seven or eight miles. Huge trunks of oak are exposed from time to time by the action of the tides, relics of the primæval forest which in a remote antiquity clothed the land. The timber is perfectly sound and serviceable ; much of it has been recovered and turned to good use. It is not discoloured like bog oak, but retains its natural hue quite fresh.

The method of recovering this valuable timber is peculiar. When a trunk becomes partly exposed, empty barrels are lashed to it at low tide, which serve to raise it out of the ooze when the tide flows again. Among other objects brought to light in this operation have been many antlers of red deer that roamed the forest thousands of years ago. Some of them are cast horns, others have portions of the skull still attached to them, suggesting that these deer had perished in the floods that swept the oaks into the bay. The size and weight of these antlers are far in excess of what may be seen in a modern and treeless Scottish deer-forest, for the red-deer being naturally a woodland animal thriving in warmth and shelter, has greatly deteriorated, not only in bulk of body, but in size and thickness of horn, since being forced to retreat before agricultural and other human industry

H

and to occupy the bleakest and most exposed parts of our island. The twentieth century sportsman may gaze with unavailing envy upon these trophies of an age long bygone; they cannot now be matched in any Highland forest, nor is there any stag on Scottish hills to-day with a frame that could support these mighty antlers, even if it had the bodily vigour to produce them.

One of these antlers lies before me as I write; it weighs seven pounds; the pair, therefore, formed a load of 14 lbs. The leverage of this load at the end of a long neck must have been formidable, especially as the tray or triple terminal cusp is the heaviest part. This antler measures 37 inches between burr and tray. It has been borne by an "imperial" stag for it has seven points, the tray measuring 14 inches long, and the beam between brow and tray is $7\frac{1}{2}$ inches in circumference. This was a live horn; another, recovered from the same part of the river, has been a cast horn. It also has seven tines, but is the moiety of a wilder head, the tray being no less than 18 inches long. Grand beasts these must have been, full-fed and nurtured in the warm forest, only repairing to the hill-tops in the heat of summer to escape the torment of flies. Dimensions such as these can never be attained by stags banished to the heights the year through, to gather a living from the hungry mountain pasture. In 1913 a remarkable exhibition of the antlers of red and fallow deer was organised by *Country Life* and arranged by the well-known taxidermists, Messrs Rowland Ward. It afforded a unique opportunity of comparing the extremes of dimension in the antlers of the red stag—the fantastic exuberance developed in sheltered quarters with abundant food, as in the head of the great Warnham stag with thirty-nine points—the baneful effect of short commons and severe exposure, as in the antlers from Loch Maddy and Corrour forest—the noble development of head-gear in British red deer acclimatised to the rich pasture and genial sunshine of New Zealand.

It is one of the mysteries of natural history why a pair of cored horns should serve an ox or an antelope throughout its life, whereas the solid antlers of a wapiti or a red stag have to be grown afresh painfully and with much irritation each succeeding summer, only to drop off in the following spring. Why should all this good material be squandered ? One is tempted to exclaim with Christ's disciples—" To what purpose is this waste ? "

Well, the wild red deer of Galloway are no more. Their former abundance and the pursuit of them is commemorated in several Gaelic place names, for Gaelic was the language of the people of Galloway in the olden times, and place-names endure long after those who bestowed them have passed away. Both the form and sense of vocables in Erse or old Gaelic differ from those of Gaelic as now spoken and written ; it is hardly possible to decide whether, for instance, such a name as Craigenveoch means the crag of the stag—*fiach*, or of the raven—*fitheaich* ; but Kilhilt (formerly written Kylnahelt), Carneltoch and Craignelder, probably signify the wood, the rock and the crag of the hinds—*eilidh* genitive plural *eilte*. Within the bounds of the ancient Forest of Buchan, extending from Glentrool to Dalmellington, we seem to catch an echo of the chase in such names as Shalloch o' Minnoch, preserving the sound of the old Gaelic *sealg*,* and Mulwharker probably stands for *maol adhairce* (pronounced " aharky "), the hill of the hunting horn.

We have the testimony of Walter Macfarlane, who died in 1767 after compiling a quantity of very interesting topographical notes now preserved in the Advocates' Library, to prove that there were plenty of red deer in the Galloway hills during the first half of the eighteenth century. About the Merrick, 2750 feet, he wrote as follows :—

*We know from written records that the ground to the west of Edinburgh Castle, now called Drumsheugh, used to be spelt Drumshelch, from the Gaelic *druim sealg*, being kept as a chace by King David I., where, to quote Bellenden's translation of Boece (xii. 16), was " an gret forest full of hartis, hyndis, toddis [foxes] and siclike manner of beastis."

" In the remote parts of this great mountain are very large Red Deer, and about the top thereof that fine bird called the Mountain Partridge or, by the commonalty, the Tarmachan, about the size of a Red Cock (grouse), and in flesh much of the same nature ; feeds, as that bird doth, on the seeds of the bullrush, and makes its protection in the chinks and hollow places of thick stones from the insults of the eagles, which are in plenty, both the large gray and the black, about that mountain."

Tradition affirms that the last red stag in the Forest of Buchan was shot by the minister of Kirkinner in 1747, four years after Mac-Queen of Pall-a-chrocain killed the last wolf on the Monadhliath among the head waters of the Findhorn. It is true that there are red deer still in an enclosure of some two thousand acres at Lord Galloway's place Cumloden. These, however, are not descended from the native stock, but from deer introduced early in the nineteenth century.* In the shelter of that well-wooded park the stags grow to great weight and carry fine heads. An untoward incident deprived me of the only chance I ever had of grassing an " imperial," that is, a stag with fourteen points. A deer-drive had been arranged, and I took the post assigned me under a low dry-stone dyke. I was not alone, for the ladies had come with us to watch the sport, and one of them was good enough to bear me company. The beaters were not yet in sight when I saw a magnificent stag moving slowly straight towards me. I told my companion that there was a fine beast coming to us ; she looked over the wall ; a large blue bow on her hat flapped in the wind, and although the stag was still a quarter of a mile from us, he caught sight of the alarm-signal, changed his direction and was shot by the rifle ensconced on our left.

As for the ptarmigan whereof Macfarlane speaks, an old shepherd in Glentrool told me long ago that they disappeared from this

---

*The red deer which, I am informed, frequent the woods of Richorn, near Dalbeattie, doubtless have a similar origin.

southern upland in 1827—" the year of the short corn "—when the drought was so severe that the oats were too short for the sickle and were pulled by hand.

The gray and the black eagles described as persecuting the ptarmigan were the erne or white-tailed eagle and the golden eagle. Their memory is preserved in the name Benyellary, a hill in height nearly equal to the Merrick, which represents the Gaelic *beinn iolare,* the eagle's hill. The last pair of golden eagles that reared their young in Galloway did so in 1835 ; but the erne had an eyrie as late as 1862. The diligence of gamekeepers has prevailed against that fine bird, which has not been recorded in the district since that year ; but in 1905 a pair of golden eagles built an eyrie on Cairnsmore-of-Fleet, failing to hatch the solitary egg laid therein. One of the pair was shot near Kirkcudbright in the following winter.

Shepherds and game-preservers may cherish no desire for the return of these formidable birds of ravin to their immemorial haunts on Benyellary, the Lum o' the Gutter and the Dungeon o' Buchan ; but for the artist and the field naturalist a soaring eagle is the one feature required to perfect the savage grandeur of Glen Trool.

Herbert Maxwell

Lt.-Col. George Eyre Todd, F.S.A., Scot.

Some Royal Hunters of the Highland Deer

By GEORGE EYRE-TODD, F.S.A., Scot.

FROM the earliest times the red deer of the hills appears to have been regarded in this country, not only as the monarch of the wild, but as the quarry most appropriate for the royal chase. For this the reason is not far to seek. With his branching crown of antlers, his stately step, his love of the clean spaciousness and freedom of the bens, and his refusal to herd at ease with stall-fed beasts, the red deer stag on his native heath looks exactly what he is, " every inch a king." A glance at his bearing is enough. He has no need even to have it written of him, as is written of a famous clan, " Is Rioghal mo dhream!" At the same time the difficulties of the deer-hunt, and the courage and resource necessary for the pursuit and attack of the monarch of the glens in his mountain fastnesses, have always made the chase of the stag peculiarly a sport of kings. In any case, if the earliest traditions and written records are to be believed, the time of the rulers of ancient Caledonia was divided chiefly between the making of war and the hunting of the deer. It is interesting, moreover, to discover to what a remote period these traditions and written allusions carry the custom back.

Possibly we shall never know who Fingal really was, the mighty warrior regarding whom and his heroes so many place-names and legends are to be found throughout the Highlands. He may have been simply the Fionn-gall, fair stranger, or Norseman, who for five centuries fought the Dubh-gall, dark stranger, or Irish Gael, for possession of the whole country west and north of the Grampians. But, whoever he was, Fingal was a mighty hunter. The great boulder below Dunnollie on Oban Bay, to which they say he tied his dog Bran, is only one of the many landmarks associating him with the chase. These legends are confirmed by the fragments of Ossianic poetry to be found in the sixteenth-century Dean of Lismore's Book and other ancient collections.

A curious allusion in these poems, further associating the Fingalian heroes with the hunting of the deer, was pointed out by the much-discussed James Macpherson and by the late Dr. Hately Waddell. When a hero is about to die he calls for his deer's horn. The meaning of this demand Macpherson declared himself unable to elucidate. But Dr. Waddell found a clue in the records of the opening of graves in the stone circles of Arran by Dr. James Bryce in 1863. Among the human remains in these tombs Dr. Bryce again and again found fragments of deer's horn. Is it possible that these fragments were trophies of the prowess of the dead hunter intended to introduce him with credit to the Happy Hunting Grounds of a future existence? This would testify the high esteem in which ability in the hunting of the red deer was held as long ago at least as the sixth century, when the Norsemen and the Gael both began their invasion of these shores.

Tokens of the hunting tastes of the Scottish kings of later centuries are numerous enough. When Queen Victoria and the Prince Consort took up residence at Balmoral in the middle of the nineteenth century they were only renewing the ancient royal vogue of the magnificent upper valley of the Dee. Castleton of Braemar takes its name, not from the curiously turreted Old Mar Castle which stands on a haugh of the Dee some distance below the village, but from an older castle of which only slight fragments remain near the end of the bridge. This stronghold is said to have been a hunting seat of Malcolm III., the great Ceannmore of the eleventh century, who overthrew Macbeth, and planted himself and a new dynasty on the Scottish throne. From the tradition it is apparent that Malcolm was a devotee of the royal sport for which the ancient Forest of Mar in the region of the upper Dee has always been famous.

But the stronghold which gave the name to Castleton of Braemar had already been the hunting seat of a much earlier king. Craig Coinnich, or Kenneth, which rises close above the spot, takes its name from an early Scottish monarch who had his hunting seat there. Until the middle of last century it was every year the scene of an athletic contest said to have been started by Kenneth himself. The contest was a race to the top of the crag, and the prize was a complete Highland costume. The finest athletes were taxed to the utmost by the effort, and sometimes showed distressing effects. For this reason the competition was stopped by Queen Victoria after she had witnessed its results.

It seems uncertain which of the Kenneths it was who came to Braemar for the fostering of manly sports and the hunting of the deer. Kenneth MacAlpin, otherwise King Kenneth I., was the eldest brother of that Gregor who is claimed as ancestor by the clan of that name. He is chiefly famous for his great victory over the Picts in 838 on the link of the Forth below Stirling, which is still known as Cambuskenneth from that fact. Eight years after the battle he succeeded to the Pictish crown. He it was who brought the Stone of Destiny and the seat of Government from Dunstaffnage to Scone, and transferred the metropolis of the Columban church, with the bones of Columba himself, from Iona to Tayside.

Kenneth II. came a century later. The son of Malcolm I., he was a great extender of his kingdom, secured Edwin's Burgh, now Edinburgh, from the Angles, and " gave the great city of Brechin to the Lord." He it was who, in the year 990, overthrew the invading Danes at the famous battle of Luncarty, near Perth, if that battle ever was fought, as the historian Boece narrates ; and five years afterwards in romantic fashion he became the victim of

I

Fenella's treacherous plot. Kenneth had slain Fenella's son for the commission of an atrocious crime, and his successful attempt to secure the immediate succession to the throne for his own son, Malcolm, threatened to oust two of Fenella's friends who were due to succeed first by the usual law of tanistry. The lady therefore prepared a plot. When Kenneth visited her castle at Fettercairn he found in his chamber a brazen statue holding forth a golden apple. When the king took the apple from the hand of the statue he released a mechanism which shot him dead with a flight of darts. The tradition will be found recounted by John Major and Hector Boece.

One or other of these monarchs of the name of Kenneth was the sportsman who hunted the deer in the Forest of Mar, used the old stronghold on the upper Dee as his hunting seat, and gave his name to Craig Coinnich, which towers above.

The youngest son of Malcolm Ceannmore was another hunter whose exp.oits are embodied in a famous tradition. David I., while still only Prince of Strathclyde, is said to have lived at Cadzow and planted the oaks there which are the only remains of the royal hunting forests of Scotland extant at the present day. He was perhaps the greatest king that Scotland ever had, was lord of all the northern English counties, exercised a dominating influence on the politics of England, and himself set the crown on the head of Henry II. To-day he is chiefly remembered in a popular way by the saying of his remote descendant, James V., that he was a " sair sanct for the crown." King James's complaint was based on the fact that David founded many great abbeys and bishoprics, and endowed them royally with lands and other possessions. Perhaps the most famous of his many foundations was the Abbey of Holyrood, and the legend of that foundation affords the clearest evidence of King David's prowess as a hunter of the deer.

At that time the ground on which Canongate is built, and eastward from the walls of Edinburgh as far almost as Musselburgh, was a natural deer forest.   According to monkish tradition, on a certain Rood-day, the festival of the Exaltation of the Cross, King David had gone from the castle to hunt in this forest.   In the hollow between the spot where the abbey now stands and the north end of Salisbury Crags, having out-ridden his companions in pursuit of a stag, he was turned upon by the infuriated animal. Unhorsed, and on the point of being gored, he was miraculously saved by the sudden appearance of a dazzling cross, or " holy rood," which struck the deer with such terror that it turned and fled.   As a token of his gratitude and piety David founded near the spot the Abbey of the Holy Rood.   The national flag of Scotland, the silver cross of St Andrew on a blue field representing the sky, is understood to commemorate the same miraculous incident.   Whatever may be the truth of the details of this story, it seems more than likely that Holyrood Abbey commemorates some actual hunting incident which befel King David near the spot.

The Sair Sanct's descendant, King Robert the Bruce, was perhaps too much occupied with affairs of war and policy to devote much time to things of the chase, but a record exists of his joining in the hunt of the deer at one of the most crucial moments in his career.   It was after his defeat at Dalrigh, near Tyndrum, and his escape from the pursuing forces of John of Lorn by ferrying his little company across the deep narrow Lochs of Lomond near Inversnaid, in the " little boat that wald bot thresome flit."   The party was reduced to the most serious straits, and indeed on the point of actual starvation, when it happily fell in with the Earl of Lennox and a hunting retinue, who were pursuing the deer on the hills between Luss or Inveruglas and Loch Long.   So relieved were the king's men, says the chronicler, John Barbour, that they fell upon their new found friends' necks and wept for joy.   In his later years Bruce retired to the same region, and at Cardross on the Leven, near Dunbarton, solaced his sickness with hunting among the hills behind and sailing on the Firth of Clyde below.

Two hundred years later the court of James IV. was a nest of singing birds, with poets like Dunbar and Kennedy and Gavin Douglas outcrying each other in wit and melody. The king himself spoke seven languages besides his own rich and expressive Scots, and with the introduction of printing, and the dawn of science in the shape of alchemy and aviation, it was the Augustan age in Scotland. But James was not less a man of war and of the hunting field than a man of books and the arts. He took signal measures to make law obeyed in the Western Isles, and on more than one occasion himself led an expedition from the Clyde in a stout ship, well manned, with full equipment of " harnes and artaillerie, boden for weir." These journeys were lightened with occasional hunting parties, and a memorial of the fact remains in Castle Stalker, the ruin of which still stands four-square on its crag a bowshot off the Appin coast. The stronghold is said to have been built by Duncan Stewart of Appin as a secure hunting seat for his " cousin," the king, when James IV. came to pursue the deer in the hills of Lorn. Alas, too soon the warlike enterprise and hunting prowess of the chivalrous and enlightened monarch were together to come to an end, when he fell at Flodden Field in the midst of his fighting earls and abbots on the dim September day of 1513.

The hunting proclivities of James V., again, can never be forgotten while the world has time to be charmed with the tale of the immortal chase recorded in " The Lady of the Lake." There is ample reason to believe that the hunt depicted with such dewy freshness and racy spirit in that poem, is no more than the reproduction of many an actual occasion on which the gay Gudeman of Ballengeich gave his whole heart to the pursuit of the deer. We know that, when he was no more than sixteen, James planned his escape from the domination of his step-father, the Earl of Angus, and his Douglas brothers at Falkland, under the ruse of a hunting party. When the two boy grooms, Jocky Hart and another, who was really the king himself, made their way to the stables in the dusk of the evening it was on the pretext of preparing the horses for the hunt on the morrow. As James galloped over Stirling bridge in the grey of the morning, and bade the gates be closed against the Douglas pursuit, he must have laughed to think how successfully he had for once changed places with the mountain quarry, and played the part of the escaping stag. Some of his later huntings in Ettrick Forest and Liddesdale were partly pretexts for the visiting of ruthless justice on Border reivers like Cockburn of Henderland and the famous Johnnie Armstrong, and remain enshrined in some of the best known Border ballads. But James knew how to turn even a lawless depredator into a friend, and the story of his dealing with Buchanan of Arnprior when that personage had commandeered the vension intended for the king's own table, shows him to have had the true spirit of a sportsman. When James, with such startling promptitude, knocked at Buchanan's gate and announced that the King of Scotland had come to dine with the "King of Kippen," the terror of the delinquent must have been qualified to some extent by the wit of the message.

James's daughter, the beautiful girl-queen, Mary Stewart, amply inherited her father's spirit. When she rode into the north to instal her ungrateful half-brother in the earldom of Moray, thus alienating her best friends, the Gordons, she declared that she wished she were a man, " to wear jack and knapscull and sleep in the fields ; " and there are constant records of her riding out in pursuit of the deer. With her husband, the vain and fickle Darnley, she visited Drummond Castle more than once to enjoy the chase in the neighbouring royal deer forest of Glenartney ; and once at least she spent some days at the Castle of Dunoon with her favourite half-sister, the Countess of Argyll, to enjoy the shooting at the butts on the castle lawn and the hawking and hunting in the glens of Cowal above the Holy Loch and Loch Eck. Those were perhaps Queen Mary's happiest days in Scotland. She could not forsee that the Countess of Argyll was to be one of the supper party present with her in the chamber at Holyrood when Darnley and his ruffians burst in and slew her secretary Rizzio at her feet. And she could not foretell that, a little later, through the cowardice or treachery of Argyll himself, her last hopes of life and fortune were to be overthrown at the battle of Langside.

James VI., Queen Mary's son, it has been the fashion to describe as the king who " never said a foolish thing, and never did a wise one." And this view of him has somewhat too effectively been stereotyped by Sir Walter Scott in " The Fortunes of Nigel." The one serious shadow on his character remains his unaccountable heedlessness of his mother's long imprisonment at the hands of Elizabeth, and his lack of indignation and prompt measures at her death. But he was Darnley's son, and it had been deeply instilled into him by George Buchanan and his other mentors that Mary was guilty of that poor creature's death. He had also, no doubt, the faults of character of Darnley and his race, the Lennox Stewarts, which he handed on, and which largely account for the faults and misfortunes of his descendants, Charles I. and the later Stewart kings. But James more than held his own with dark and unscrupulous schemers like Gowrie and Morton and Mar in a most difficult time in Scotland, and probably no one else of all our princes could so well have served the purposes of peace between the kingdoms at the delicate crisis of the union of the crowns. It is interesting therefore to find that James also was a sportsman. It is enough to cite the fact that he was setting out from Falkland for the hunt when Alexander Ruthven brought him the message which induced him to leave the field and gallop away, with a small retinue or none, to encounter the strange adventure in Gowrie House at Perth, which has remained a mystery till the present day.

From the time of James VI. Scotland saw but little of her kings for two hundred years. Charles I. paid a couple of strenuous political visits to the north. Charles II., just after his father's death, "enjoyed," under the strict supervision of the Covenanters, a few month's sovereignty which came to an abrupt end with the battle of Dunbar. In the only hunting in which he took part on that occasion he was himself the quarry, when he managed to escape from his mentors as far as Clova in the Grampians, only to be brought back in a day or two to a more exasperating sur-veillance. His brother, afterwards James VII. and II., was for a time, while Duke of York, at the head of the Scottish Government, but he was too busy with the policy which afterwards brought about the Revolution and his final loss of the crown, to devote time to such healthy open-air pursuits as the hunting of the red deer. And of all the huntings that ever took place in Scotland that of James VII.'s grandson, "bonnie Prince Charlie," was certainly the most romantic and exciting; but it had nothing whatever to do with stag or hind. George IV., again, paid his famous visit to Scotland in 1824, but modern deer-stalking was not yet then a fashion, and the " First Gentleman in Europe " was in any case likely to be intent on the social pleasures of the Scottish capital rather than on any pursuit requiring more than a modicum of physical exertion.

It was not till the middle of the nineteenth century that the hunting of the Highland deer again received a royal imprimatur. In her " Leaves from the Journal of our Life in the Highlands " on 8th September, 1848, Queen Victoria wrote, " We arrived at Balmoral at a quarter to three. It is a pretty little castle in the old Scottish style. There is a picturesque tower and garden in front, with a high wooded hill ; at the back there is a wood down to the Dee ; and the hills rise all around." The Queen and the Prince Consort, eager as children with a new plaything, "lunched almost immediately," sallied forth afterwards and walked about the place, regarding which the Queen was full of delight. Then she continues, " When I came in at half-past-six, Albert went out to try his luck with some stags which lay quite close in the woods, but he was unsuccessful. They come down of an evening quite near to the house."

Such was the beginning of the new royal resort to Deeside. The Queen had bought the remaining twenty-seven years of Sir Robert Gordon's lease of Balmoral from the Earl of Fife. In 1852 the estate was purchased outright by the Prince Consort, who proceeded in the following year to build the present castle, and there every autumn for nearly half a century he and the Queen, and the widowed Queen alone after his death, resorted for a couple of month's holiday among the deer forests and the grouse moors. Many august and distinguished guests were entertained; the chief sport was the stalking of the deer in the surrounding hills; and from that royal example the vogue spread which has made the bare mountainsides and lonely glens and corries to-day the most fashionable sporting region in the world.

King Edward, both when Prince of Wales, living at Abergeldie and afterwards as king at Balmoral itself, was one of the most enthusiastic and successful stalkers of the deer. The late William Simpson, well-known as " Crimean Simpson," the first war artist, who stayed once at Abergeldie as the Prince's guest, has, in his fascinating autobiography, left an account of a day's deer-stalking there. " The day before I left," he says, " the Prince went deer-stalking, and took me with him. We first drove in a trap past Balmoral, where we met the Queen walking on the grass. The Prince stopped the trap, and I remember that the conversation was about President Garfield (just then assassinated). The Queen had had a telegram that morning announcing his death, and the two royal personages spoke very feelingly about the event. After driving some distance to the west of the castle, we had ponies to go up part of the hill. At last we left the ponies, and the stalking began.   Some deer were seen, and a shot or two were fired. As we walked over the moor the Prince picked up a bit of white heather, and, presenting it to me, said, ' There's a piece of white heather to you for good luck.'   We lunched high up, near the summit of Loch-na-gar.   Afterwards we went on, and at last came down upon Altnaguisach, where we had tea.   Letters and telegrams were here waiting the Prince.   There was only one large trap to bring us back to Abergeldie, and into it the Prince, myself. and the ghillies went. We were rather crammed. His Royal Highness started me to tell the ghillies about the tiger-shooting when the Prince was in India, which interested them very much.   When we set out in the morning a stick, a long one with a crook at the end, such as deer-stalkers use in the hills, had been lent to me. On my return in the evening the Prince told me to preserve it as a souvenir of the day.   I afterwards had a silver ring put on it, with an inscription."

Following King Edward, His Majesty King George, as all the world knows, spends a few weeks each autumn with the Queen at what has come to be the Highland home of the Royal Family of these realms ; and each autumn, in pursuit of the deer on the slopes of Lochnagar, or in the royal forest of Ballochbuie, renews his energies for the arduous and anxious life of a ruler in these times, and renews as well the ancient associations of the kings of the Scots with this Royal sport in those remote fastnesses of the Grampians and the Dee.

George Eyre-Todd.

K

APPENDIX I.

The Deer Forests of Scotland

Lament of the Stag Royal

By the regal crest that crowns me,
  By the scars that speak of men ;
By the well-filled hide that gowns me,
  I am chieftain of the glen.
By the herdship right that thrones me,
  I am lord of field and flood ;
Not a hart or hind but owns me,
  By my antler'd badge of blood.

In the veins that run to drain me
  It was ancient blood that ran ;
In the pulsing racks that pain me
  I can can feel the teeth of Bran !
Not a lone buck dares to flout me,
  Not a herd hind dares resist ;
I am lord of all about me—
  I am Monarch of the Mist !

In the gloaming gloom that hides me,
  'Neath the beetling of the ben,
I have crawled where none derides me ;
  I shall die in no one's ken.
Fatal fast my hurts are welling,
  Laboured now my failing breath ;
With the eagles round me yelling,
  I am brought to bay—with death !

Oh ! the hazel glades that laired me.
  Oh ! the moonlight pools I knew !
And the soft-eyed hinds that dared me
  When the rutting times were new !
Flicker past old scenes before me,
  Ere my crown was marked of men ;
Fawnhood days when young blood bore me,
  Fleeting far by glade and glen.

One last look ere sight shall fail me,
  One proud look on realms of mine ;
Let me see ere men shall trail me,
  Hills and hollows, birch and pine,
Silent strath, loch, glen, and corrie,
  Heather, bracken, moor, and moss ;
Mine the pride and mine the glory,
  But in Death now—mine the loss !

TRAMP ROYAL.

Off the Beaten Track with the Rifle

A Typical West Highland Forest

TENNENT'S

TRADE MARK

ESTABLISHED
1745

ORIGINALLY FOUNDED
1556

LAGER BEER

WELLPARK BREWERY, GLASGOW

The Deer Forests of Scotland

ABERDEENSHIRE.

ABERGELDIE AND WHITEMOUNTH (16,010 acres). *Prop.*—His Majesty The King.

BACHNAGAIRN AND GLENMUICK (28,531 acres). *Prop.*—Sir Victor A. F. Mackenzie, Bart.

BALMORAL AND BALLOCHBUIE (23,991 acres). *Prop.*—His Majesty The King.

BIRKHALL. *Prop.*—His Majesty The King.

GLENCALLATER (10,147 acres). *Prop.*—A. H. Farquharson of Invercauld. Lessee—Major Morel.

GLENTANNAR (27,725 acres). *Prop.*—Lord Glentannar.

INVERCAULD (45,000 acres). *Prop.*—A. Farquharson. Lessee—Herbert Johnson. Agent—A. Smith, Invercauld.

MAR (87,196 acres). *Prop.*—Trustees of the late Duke of Fife

ARGYLLSHIRE.

ARDLUSSA (22,012 acres). *Prop.*—The North Jura Co., Ltd. Lessee—Lord Claude Hamilton.

ARDNAMURCHAN (26,160 acres). *Prop.*—Kenneth M. Clarke. Lessee— T. O. M. Sopwith.

ARDTORNISH, MORVERN (12,392 acres). *Prop.*—C. Craig Sellar, Esq.

BENMORE (MULL) (19,430 acres). *Prop.*—The Duke of Argyll. Lessee —H. G. Younger.

BLACKCORRIES (18,125 acres). *Prop.*—Lady Strathcona and Mount Royal.

BLACKMOUNT (70,000 acres). *Prop.*—The Trustees of the late Marquess of Breadalbane. Lessees—Major R. Fleming, Ian T. Nelson, Esq., V. R. Balfour-Browne, Esq. Average for past 5 years—105 Stags, 80 brace Grouse and B. Game. In 1924 there were 10 Royals got on the Forest, and the heaviest stag was 18 st. 10 lbs. This magnificent Forest was broken up into three portions in 1924. Previously shot by the late Marquess of Breadalbane. There is excellent fishing in the Rivers Orchy and Kinglas, including Salmon, Sea Trout, and Brown Trout. The hill lochs, which are strictly preserved, also afford excellent sport. Agent—James Campbell, Killin.

CONAGLEN (16,981 acres). *Prop.*—The Earl of Morton.

CRAIG (27,000 acres). *Prop.*—The Trustees of the late Marquess of Breadalbane. Lessee—Leslie Garton, Esq., Hollyhill, Banstead, Surrey. Average for past 5 years—51 Stags, 40 brace Grouse, and a good bag of low ground game. In 1924 there was one Royal, one 13-pointer, four 11-pointers, eleven 10-pointers; heaviest stag, 18 st. 17 lbs. There is excellent salmon fishing in the River Orchy, and 50 Salmon in a season is the usual basket. The hill lochs also afford excellent sport. Agent—James Campbell, Killin.

DALNESS (11,640 acres). *Prop.*—The Trustees of the late the Honourable Sir Schomberg Kerr McDonnell. Lessee—The Right Honourable Margaret Charlotte Lady Strathcona and Mount Royal (on lease). Average—30 Stags, 30 Hinds. Agent—J. W. E. Steedman, S.S.C., Royal Bank Buildings, Oban.

GLENETIVE (10,339 acres). *Prop.*—Ian T. Nelson of Glenetive.

GLENFORSA (2,227 acres). *Prop.*—Col. A. D. Greenhill-Gardyne.

GLENFYNE FOREST, ARDKINGLAS (20,000 acres). *Prop.*—Sir John Noble, Bart. Average—35 Stags, 20 Hinds. Two Royals 1924; heaviest 22 st., average 16/17 st. Agent—R. R. Ballingall, Ardkinglas Estate Office, Inveraray.

GLENLECKNAMUIE (GLENCOE) (2,026 acres). *Prop.*—Lady Strathcona and Mount Royal.

Scottish Deer Forests

Estates,
Shootings & Fishings.

Register published Annually.

GROUSE
MOORS

SALMON
FISHINGS

Walker, Fraser & Steele
ESTATE AGENTS

AGENTS for all the principal Forests, Grouse Moors, Mixed Shootings, and Fishings in Scotland available each season to let and for sale.

The Scottish Register, *the most comprehensive list of above published, is obtainable on application.*

Head Office: 74 Bath Street, Glasgow

TELEGRAMS: SPORTSMAN, GLASGOW
Telephones - - 660 Douglas (2 Lines)

Duke of Portland on his Caithness estates, Langwell and Braemore. The average number per annum for the last twenty years is 104, and the average weight 14 st. 13 lbs. The heaviest during that period were :—17th Sept., 1902, 23 st. 2 lbs.; 28th Sept., 1912, 22 st. 2 lbs.; 28th Aug., 1924, 23 st. 4 lbs.; 2nd Oct., 1924, 22 st. 2 lbs.—all killed by His Grace. In the war years, 1914-1918, there were killed in Langwell and Braemore 608 Stags and 934 Hinds,

HIS GRACE THE DUKE OF PORTLAND.

the venison being given to the Red Cross. A considerable number of Sheep and Cattle are grazed in the Forest. Agent—J. Harling Turner, Portland Estate Office, Kilmarnock.

SANDSIDE (13,050 acres). *Prop.*—Allan D. Pilkington. Lessee—Thos. Pilkington.

DUMBARTONSHIRE.

LOCH SLOY (14,055 acres). *Prop.*—Trustees of the late Alan J. Colquhoun of Colquhoun and Luss, Bart. Lessee—Sir Iain Colquhoun, Bart. Average

Sport and the Weather

The Sportsman depends for enjoyment on protection from the weather, and British weather is proverbially uncertain—impossible to foretell what it is likely to be from one day to another.

Don't take chances ; be prepared, wear

THE
BURBERRY

THE BRITISH COAT THAT DEFIES BRITISH WEATHER

It keeps the wearer perfectly dry in heavy rain

Healthfully warm when there's a cold wind blowing

Cool and comfortable on close, but moist, days

Easy-fitting, airylight, thin and flexible, The Burberry makes no difference to the "set" of the gun at the shoulder, and is the ONE Weatherproof in which the good "shot" can maintain his form completely protected against wind and wet instead of finding bad weather destructive of his reputation.

Illustrated Catalogue & Patterns Post Free

Every Burberry Garment is labelled "Burberrys"

BURBERRYS LTD. HAYMARKET LONDON S.W.1

C

pointer weighing 17 st. 10 lb.　On the 10th September Miss Gwen grassed a ten-pointer weighing 17 st. 8 lb., and on the same day Miss Edith brought down an eight-pointer weighing 14 st.　On the 22nd September, in the West Pass of Deaces, Miss Gwen, after a long and arduous stalk, secured a 19 stoner.　It had nine points, and was taken on the gallop at 120 yards.　It was the record weight for several years.　Both ladies used .240 rifles.

MISS GWEN LATILLA.

GLENCALLY (2,122 acres).　*Prop.*—Andrew G. K Smyth.

GLENDOLL (8,621 acres).　*Prop.*—Duncan Macpherson.

GLENISLA (700 acres).　*Prop.*—John P. Gibb.

HUNTHILL (15,000 acres).　*Prop.*—Rt. Hon. The Earl of Dalhousie. Lessee—Mr Baker, New York.　Average—25 Stags.　Stag 21 st. got in 1923.　Agent—Samuel Edwards, Brechin.

INVERMARK (26,500 acres).　*Prop.*—Rt. Hon. The Earl of Dalhousie. Brechin Castle, Brechin.　Average 70-80 Stags.　Mr Sam. Edwards, factor to the Earl of Dalhousie, brought down a magnificent specimen of a stag whilst shooting over the Hunthill Deer Forest, which is on Lord Dalhousie's estate,

and is presently leased by Mr George F. Baker, of New York. The Stag scaled 21 st. clean weight—an exceptionally heavy animal. The head, a nine-pointer, was strong and wild; the body was beautifully proportioned; altogether a very fine specimen. Agent—Samuel Edwards, Brechin.

INVERNESS-SHIRE.

ABERARDER (9,245 acres). *Prop.*—A. C. Macpherson of Cluny. Lessee —W. G. Clegg.

ABERNETHY (21,408 acres). *Prop.*—Trustees of the late Countess Dowager of Seafield. Lessee—R. H. Holt.

ACHDALIEU (6,048 acres). *Prop.*—Col. Donald Cameron of Lochiel. Lessee—Mrs Parsons.

ACHNACARRY (32,429 acres). *Prop.*—Col. Donald Cameron of Lochiel. Lessees—North, Major Birkin; South, N. McCorquodale.

AFFARIC (34,000 acres). *Prop.*—Trustees of the late Mrs Chisholm of Chisholm, Erchless Castle, Strathglass. Lessee—The Right. Hon. Lord Furness of Grantley, Yorkshire. Average—80 Stags. Fully stocked with heavy Deer, many Stags being Royals. The two best heads of season 1921 have been credited to the Chisholm Forests—one, a very fine 11-pointer, being got on Affaric. There are also the usual varieties of Game. Agents—Messrs Innes & Mackay, Solicitors, Inverness.

ALVIE (3,264 acres). *Prop.*—R. B. Whitehead. Lessee—Countess of Carnarvon.

AMHUINNSUIDH (36,125 acres). *Prop.*—The Lewis and Harris Welfare and Development Co., Ltd.

ARDVERIKIE (37,000 acres). *Prop.*—Sir John F. Ramsden, Bart., of Ardverikie, Kingussie. Lessee—J. S. Phipps, Esq., New York, U.S.A. Average—100 Stags; largest number killed in one season, 144. The average weight of Stags killed in this Forest for the past number of years is 15 st. 3 lb., the heaviest being one weighing 24 st. 7 lb. Many striking heads have been got. Several years ago a head was secured by Lord Inveagh of 17 points, the measurements of which were—Length of horn, $34\frac{1}{4}$ in.; span inside, 29 in.; girth, $4\frac{3}{4}$ in. Another outstanding head was secured by Mr E. J. Wythes in 1909, a Royal measuring—Length, $39\frac{1}{2}$ in.; span inside, 25 in.; girth, 5 in. Agent—Alex. Mackay, Gallovie, Kingussie.

ARISAIG AND RHU (11,875 acres). *Prop.*—Sir Arthur W. Nicholson.

A2

ARNISDALE (9,000 acres).   *Prop.*—Sir John Harmood Banner, Bart., Ingmire Hall, Sedbergh, Yorkshire. Average—25 Stags, 30 Hinds.   20 Salmon ,200 to 300 Sea Trout, 300 to 400 Brown Trout.   2 Royals, 4 10's, 1924. Agent—J. Macrae, Mallaig.

BALMACAAN (24,220 acres).   *Prop.*—Trustees of the late Countess Dowager of Seafield.   Lessee—Col. Jenkins.

BEN ALDER (23,000 acres).   *Prop.*—Sir John F. Ramsden, Bart., of Ardverikie, Kingussie.   Previous Lessee—E. J. Wythes, Esq., London. Average—90 Stags.   The average weight of Stags killed is just over 15 st., and weights go up to over 20 st.   In each season several Royals are secured, and one strong, rough head, a nine-pointer, got two years ago, measured as follows :—Length of horn, $33\frac{1}{2}$ in.; span inside, $32\frac{1}{2}$ in.; girth, $5\frac{1}{8}$ in.   An eleven-pointer head was got in 1923, on which the '' tops '' measured 11 in. Agent—Alex. Mackay, Gallovie, Kingussie.

BRAEROY (21,000 acres).   *Prop.*—Sir John F. Ramsden, Bart., of Ardverikie, Kingussie.   Lessee—R. L. Scott, Esq., Greenock.   Average—50 Stags.   The average weight of Stags killed in this Forest is $15\frac{1}{2}$ st.; weights go up to $20\frac{1}{2}$ st.   Many good heads have been secured, up to 14 points.   In one season seven Royals were killed.   A head secured is interesting on account of the exceptionally heavy brow antlers, these being $15\frac{3}{4}$ in. long; the horn itself was $36\frac{1}{2}$ in. long. Agent—Alex. Mackay, Gallovie, Kingussie.

CAMUSUNARY AND CORUISK (13,546 acres).   *Prop.*—W. L. Johnson and MacLeod of MacLeod.

CEANNACROC (27,600 acres).   *Prop.* Glenmoriston Estates, Ltd.   Lessee —Sir V. Warrender, Bart.

COIGNAFEARN (31,756 acres).   *Prop.*—Mackintosh of Mackintosh.   Lessee —A. Cross.

CORRIMONY (10,730 acres).   *Prop.*—Mrs Elizabeth Macpherson.   Lessee —H. Bateson.

CORROUR (56,857 acres).   *Prop.*—Sir John Stirling Maxwell. Bart.

CORRYARRICK (OR DRUMIN) (6,724 acres).   *Prop.*—Sir John F. Ramsden, Bart.   Lessee—Major R. S. Nairn.

CULACHY (8,262 acres).   *Prop.*—Mrs M. Beckett.   Lessee—I. N. Horlick.

DORLIN (8,467 acres).   *Prop.*—Lord Howard of Glossop.   Lessee—Sir A. H. Maguire.

G. & G. Ponton

MACHINE PHOTOGRAVURE PRINTERS
IN COLOUR AND MONOCHROME
BY THE "PONTOPRINT" PROCESS

468 CATHEDRAL STREET,
GLASGOW.

DUNMAGLASS (12,500 acres). *Prop.*—Major T. P. Barber, D.S.O. Agent—E. G. Critchley, Inverness.

ERCHLESS (12,000 acres). *Prop.*—Trustees of the late Mrs Chisholm of Chisholm, Erchless Castle, Strathglass. Lessee—E. H. Litchfield, Esq., 111 Broadway, New York, U.S.A. Average—30 Stags. In addition to Deer, the usual varieties of game are obtained, viz.—Grouse, Black Game, Snipe, Duck, Pheasants, Partridges, Woodcock, etc. Agents—Messrs Innes & Mackay, Solicitors, Inverness.

FASNAKYLE (25,000 acres). *Prop.*—Trustees of the late Mrs Chisholm of Chisholm, Erchless Castle, Strathglass. Lessee—Colonel Stephenson R. Clarke of Borde Hill, Cuckfield, Sussex. Average—60 Stags. Fasnakyle, which has been tenanted by Colonel Clarke for many years, has been carefully nursed and lightly shot by him. It is fully stocked with heavy deer, many stags being Royals. In 1921 a fine Imperial was got by the tenant. Agents—Messrs Innes & Mackay, Solicitors, Inverness.

GAICK (20,000 acres). *Prop.*—Sir George Macpherson Grant, Bart., Ballindalloch. Lessee—Robert Hargreaves, Esq. (Forest has been let to same family for the past 52 seasons). Average—60 Stags.

GARRYGOULACH (12,480 acres). *Prop.*—Major E. C. Ellice.

GLENCANNICH (15,000 acres). *Prop.*—Trustees of the late Mrs Chisholm of Chisholm, Erchless Castle, Strathglass. Lessee—Mrs Milburn, 22 Lennox Gardens, London, S.W.1. Average—40 Stags. Splendid stalking ground. There are also Grouse, Black Game, Ptarmigan, Duck, and other game. Agents—Messrs Innes & Mackay, Solicitors, Inverness.

GLENDOE (20,947 acres). *Prop.*—Philip E. Noble. Lessee—Mr Bideaux.

GLENFESHIE (37,000 acres). *Prop.*—Sir George Macpherson Grant, Bart. Lessee—W. Riley-Smith, Esq., Toulston, Tadcaster. Agent—C. Mackenzie, Ballindalloch Castle.

GLENFINNAN AND GLENALADALE (25,000 acres). *Prop.*—The Executors of the late Mrs Margaret MacDonald of Glenaladale. Lessee—The Right Hon. The Viscount Mountgarret. Average—70 Stags. Royal, ten-pointer, and nine-pointer shot in 1924. A place of great historic interest, where Prince Charlie raised his standard in the '45 Rebellion. Agent—Edward E. Malcolm, W.S., Fort-William.

GLENGARRY (16,905 acres). *Prop.*—Major E. C. Ellice.

GLENKINGIE (25,000 acres). *Prop.*—Col. Cameron of Lochiel. Lessee—Lord Belper. Average—45 Stags. This Forest is being very carefully shot; the heads are distinctly above the average. Agent—E. Malcolm, Fort-William.

GLENMAZERAN AND GLENKYLLACHY, TOMATIN (11,952 acres). *Prop.*—Wm. Dalziel Mackenzie of Farr. On lease for 10 years to Captain William Higson, Burton Hall, Melton Mowbray. Average—30 Stags. Glenmazeran, with Glenkyllachy, lies on the west side of the River Findhorn, in the District of Strathdearn. Excellent Deer and Grouse ground. Other game consists of Roe-deer, Blackcock, Woodcock, Snipe, Wild Duck, Hares, Rabbits, and a few Pheasants. Excellent Trout fishing on the Findhorn and Mazeran, and a few Salmon. Agents—Innes & Mackay, Inverness.

GLENMORE (12,653 acres). *Prop.*—Forestry Commissioners (Scotland) Lessee—H. G. Hambro.

GLENQUOICH (30,000 acres). *Prop.*—Major E. C. Ellice. Lessee—W. H. Cox.

GLENSHERO (21,000 acres). *Prop.*—Sir John F. Ramsden, Bart., of Ardverikie, Kingussie. Lessee—Major R. Spencer Nairn, Kirkcaldy. Average—50 Stags. The average weight of Stags killed is 15¼ st., and weights go up to 20 st. In each season several Royals are secured. Agent—Alex. Mackay, Gallovie, Kingussie.

GLENSTRATHFARAR (BRAULEN) (36,000 acres). *Prop.*—Rt. Hon. Lord Lovat, Beaufort Castle, Beauly, Inverness-shire. Lessee—Sir John Dewrance, K.B.E. Average—75 Stags. Agent—G. J. Garrioch, Lovat Estate Office, Beauly.

GUISACHAN (21,974 acres). *Prop.*—Portsmouth Estates Improvement Co., Ltd. Lessee—Col. F. C. Grant.

INSHREACH (5,021 acres). *Prop.*—Mackintosh of Mackintosh. Lessee—Mrs E. W. Clarke.

INVERAILORT (8,707 acres). *Prop.*—Mrs Cameron-Head.

INVERESHIE (6,115 acres) *Prop.*—Sir George Macpherson-Grant, Bart.

INVERLOCHY AND KILLIECHONATE (31,565 acres). *Prop.*—Trustees of the late Lord Abinger.

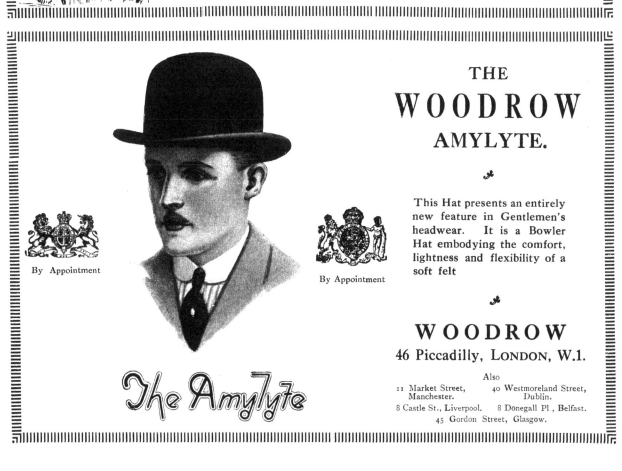

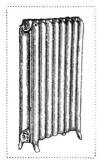

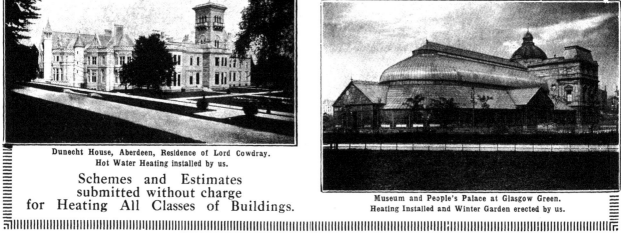

APPENDIX

13

INVERMORISTON (INCLUDING DUNDREGGAN AND LEVISHIE) (16,426 acres). *Prop.*—Glenmoriston Estates, Ltd. Lessees—Capt. Grant, T. L. Nelson, Mrs F. M. Arding.

INVERWICK (3,840 acres). *Prop.*—I. R. J. M. Grant of Glenmoriston. Lessee—Sir Thomas Roydon, Bart.

KINLOCH HOURN (6,586 acres). *Prop.*—Trustees of the late Robert Birkbeck.

KINLOCHMOIDART, GLENFINNAN (10,147 acres). *Prop.*—J. C. Stewart of Kinlochmoidart. Lessee—Rt. Hon. Lord Eglinton. Average—40 Stags, 30 Hinds. The place is for sale. Agent—E. E. Malcolm, Fort-William.

KINVEACHY (11,224 acres). *Prop.*—Trustees of the late Countess Dowager of Seafield. Lessee—P. O. Watkin Browne.

KNOYDART (48,278 acres). *Prop.*—Arthur S. Bowlby.

LANGAS (11,990 acres). *Prop.*—Sir A. J. Campbell-Orde Bart. Lessee—Lt.-Col. Anstruther Gray.

LETTERMORAR (7,075 acres). *Prop.*—Sir Berkeley Sheffield, Bart.

LUSKENTYRE (5,760 acres). *Prop.*—Lewis and Harris Welfare and Development Co., Ltd.

MAMORE (36,000 acres). *Prop.*—Lady Fairfax-Lucy of Glen Nevis and Mamore. Lessee—Captain F. B. Bibby. (Held on long lease by the late Mr F. Bibby, and now by his son since 1898). Average—100 Stags. Last year only old and bad Stags were shot.

MEOBLE (14,976 acres). *Prop.*—Sir Berkeley Sheffield, Bart.

MORAR (10,000 acres). *Prop.*—E. H. Secker, Garramore, Arisaig. Average—25 Stags, 10 Hinds. Last year, 11-pointer with good cups. Forest has been solely shot by owner for last six years, care being taken to shoot only very bad heads, or heads worth setting up.

MOY (6,044 acres). *Prop.*—Sir John F. Ramsden, Bart. Lessee—G. S. Albright.

NEWTON AND SPONISH, N. UIST (2,851 acres). *Prop.*—Sir A. J. Campbell-Orde, Bart. Average—15 Stags. At Newton in 1912 Mr J. Talbot-Clifton created a right-and-left record for Scotland by bringing down a 12-pointer (20 st. 11 lb.) and a 15-pointer (21 st. 6 lb.).

RANNACHAN (2,957 acres). *Prop.*—Mrs Cameron-Head

Rothiemurchus (with Drumintoul Lodge) (19,000 acres). *Prop.*— J. P. Grant of Rothiemurchus, Aviemore. Lessee (since 1920)—Mrs Granger Stewart, 2 Ennismore Gardens, S.W. Average—50 Stags, 80 Hinds, 200-300 brace Grouse, 100-150 brace Ptarmigan, 25 brace Black Game, 25 Caper, and good various. Heads noted more for their elegance than their size. In pre-war days the Forest used to give anything up to 70 Stags. Now, however, owing to the under-shooting of Mar and the prevalence of tourists, Stags do not come on to the ground much until fairly late in the season, when there is enough ground for three rifles. There is a lot of high ground, and Ptarmigan are very numerous; more than 60 brace were got in a day in 1924. The Grouse bag could be considerably increased if driving was done and the ground systematically burned.

Rum (25,968 acres). *Prop.*—Sir George Bulloch, Bart.

Sconser (11,233 acres). *Prop.*—The Rt. Hon. Lord Macdonald, Armadale Castle, Isle of Skye. Previous Lessee—Sir Vesey Holt. Average— 12 Stags, 6 Hinds, about 150 brace Grouse. Some Royals have been got. Contains some very good corries. Grouse and good mixed bag of game can be had. Limit of Grouse has for past few years been reduced to enable ground to recover from effect of war years. Usual limit, 250 to 300 brace. Agent— George Mackay Fraser, Portree.

Struy (18,576 acres). *Prop.*—Col. Howard Lister Cooper.

Urchany and Farley (6,000 acres). *Prop.*—Lord Lovat. Lessee— Ashley Leggatt. Average—10 Stags. A 13-pointer shot in 1924. Agent— J. T. Garrioch, Beauly.

KINCARDINESHIRE.

Glendye (14,500 acres). *Prop.*—Sir John Robert Gladstone, Bart.

KIRKCUDBRIGHTSHIRE.

Cumloden (2,524 acres). *Prop.*—The Earl of Galloway.

PERTHSHIRE.

Atholl (1, West Hand, 10,000 acres; 2, Forest Lodge Home beats, 24,000 acres). *Prop.*—Duke of Atholl. Average—(1), 60 Harts; (2), 80 Harts.

Barracks (18,902 acres). *Prop.*—Miss J. L. Robertson of Struan.

Chesthill (4,930 acres). *Prop.*—Trustees of the late Sir D. Currie. Lessees—Capt. and Mrs Wisely.

CLUNES (4,445 acres). *Prop.*—The Duke of Atholl.

CORRIEVARKIE (5,500 acres). *Prop.*—John D. Cobbold. Lessee—A. J. Brandon.

CRAGANOUR (21,515 acres). *Prop.*—John D. Cobbold. Lessee—R. Pilkington.

CROSSCRAIG AND RANNOCH (8,000 acres). *Prop.*—Drysdale Kilburn, Derby House, Hendon. Average—30 Stags, 35 Hinds, 500 brace of Grouse. A nine-pointer grassed last season. Length, 36 in.; spread; $34\frac{1}{2}$ in.; weight, clean, 17 st. 4 lb.; a fine wild head.

DALNACARDOCH AND SRONPHADRICK (16,944 acres). *Prop.*—The Duke of Atholl. Lessee—Marquis of Sligo.

DALNAMEIN (10,109 acres). *Prop.*—The Duke of Atholl. Lessee—G. W. Swire.

DALNASPIDAL (11,117 acres). *Prop.*—The Duke of Atholl. Lessee—Col. F. S. Seely.

DUNALASTAIR (8,717 acres). *Prop.*—Mrs J. de Sales la Terrière of Dunalastair. Lessee—F. Dudley Docker.

FEALAR (13,000 acres). *Prop.*—Duke of Atholl, Blair Castle. Lessee—John Calder. Average—60 Stags. Agent—M. Inglis, Blair Atholl.

GLENARTNEY (17,213 acres). *Prop.*—The Earl of Ancaster.

GLENFRUAR (11,000 acres). *Prop.*—Duke of Atholl. Average—45 Harts.

GLENLOCHSIE (6,336 acres). *Prop.*—Sir Archibald Birkmyre.

GLENLYON (5,088 acres). *Prop.*—Trustees of the late Sir D. Currie. Lessee—Mrs Molteno.

LOCHS (7,748 acres). *Prop.*—The Marquess of Breadalbane. Lessee—Sir E. S. Wills, Bart.

RANNOCH (14,093 acres). *Prop.*—John D. Cobbold. Lessee—Chas. Dempster.

TALLADH-A-BHEITHE (13,785 acres). *Prop.*—John D. Cobbold,

ROSS-SHIRE.

ACHANAULT AND STRATHBRAN (10,080 acres). *Prop.*—Captain A. T. Bignold-De Cologan, Marques de Torre Hermosa. Lessee—Frederick S. Mead, Harvard University, U.S.A. Average—25 Stags, 2 Fallow Bucks, 2 Japanese Bucks. Agents—Messrs J. Watson Lyall & Co., 21 Pall Mall.

ALINE (8,621 acres). *Prop.*—Donald Macrae. Lessee—Donald Macrae.

ALLADALE. *Prop.*—Sir Chas. Ross.

AMAT (768 acres). *Prop.*—Ird. H. Thompson. Lessee—Marquis of Conyngham.

ARDLAIR. *Prop.*—Earl of Ronaldshay.

APPLECROSS (80,000 acres). *Prop.*—Lord Middleton, Birdsall House, Malton, Yorks. Lessee—C. Vyner, Esq. Average—60 Stags. Good Royal by Hon. C. Willoughby in 1923. River—Bag, 1924—60 Salmon, 200 Sea Trout. Agent—J. Bell, Estate Office, Birdsall, Malton, Yorks.

ATTADALE (35,000 acres). *Prop.*—Captain William Schroder, late 9th Lancers, Attadale, Strathcarron. Average—35 to 40 Stags. Excellent Sea Trout fishing in River Carron. Good Salmon fishing in River Luig. Agent— T. H. Burns, M.A., solicitor, Dingwall.

BEN DAMPH (13,363 acres). *Prop.*—The Earl of Lovelace.

BENMORE (42,510 acres). *Prop.*—Sir Charles Ross, Bart. Lessees— D. & W. McLeod.

BENULA (20,000 acres). *Prop.*—Trustees of the late Mrs Chisholm of Chisholm, Erchless Castle, Strathglass. Lessees—(Part of South Benula)— Captain John Stirling of Fairburn, Muir of Ord, Ross-shire, and Duncan Alexander Stirling, Esq., London. (Part of North Benula)—William MacBean, Esq., Scotscraig, Inverness. Average—65 Stags. Fully stocked with Deer. In 1908 one Imperial and two Royals were got, in 1910 two Royals, and in 1912 five Royals. Excellent Brown Trout fishing.—Agents—Messrs Innes & Mackay, solicitors, Inverness.

BRAEMORE (42,000 acres). *Prop.*—Rev. Sir Montague Fowler, Bart., J.P., Merryhill House, Bushey, Herts. Lessee—Mr W. Hargreaves Brown. Previous Lessee—Sir Victor Warrender, Bart., M.P. Average—90 to 95 Stags (on Braemore and Inverbroom) to Mr Hargreaves Brown. Four 14-pointers have been killed in the Forest.

CASTLE LEOD. *Prop.* Countess of Cromartie. Lessee—Mrs Trench.

CLUANIE AND GLENSHIEL (30,055 acres). *Prop.*—J. E. B. Baillie of Dochfour. Lessees—C. Williams, Col. Hardcastle.

CORRIEHALLIE (6,471 acres). *Prop.*—Capt. and Mrs Frances G. Mackenzie-Gillanders of Highfield. Lessee—H. T. Ionides.

CORRIEMOILLIE (5,587 acres). *Prop.*—Mrs K. R. M. Bell. Lessee—Sir E. J. Soares.

CORRIEMULZIE (11,200 acres). *Prop.*—Ian M. Campbell.

COULIN (20,000 acres). *Prop.*—Dinam Estates Company, Llandinam. Lessee—Mr David Davies, M.P. Average for ten years—32 Stags. Agent—J. J. Borthwick, Llandinam.

DEANICH. *Prop.*—Sir Charles Ross.

DIBIEDALE (14,304 acres). *Prop.*—C. W. Dyson Perrins.

DORISDUAN AND INVERINATE (21,215 acres). *Prop.*—Sir Keith A. Fraser, Bart., Carlton Curlieu Hall, Leicester. Lessee—Capt. Hon. G. B. Portman. Average—32 Stags, 180 brace Grouse. Agents—Innes & Mackay, Inverness.

DRUMRUINIE (11,913 acres). *Prop.*—The Countess of Cromartie. Lessee—Col. Delby.

DUNDONNELL (28,119 acres). *Prop.*—H. Mackenzie of Dundonnell. Lessee—P. W. Ratcliff.

FANNICH AND GLASLET (14,784 acres). *Prop.*—Vernon J. Watney.

FLOWERDALE (10,031 acres). *Prop.*—Sir Kenneth Mackenzie, Bart. Lessee—The Hon. Sydney Peel.

FREEVATER (33,341 acres). *Prop.*—Sir Chas. Ross, Bart.

GARBAT. *Prop.*—Countess of Cromartie. Lessee—Col. R. Shoolbred.

GLENBEG AND INVERLAEL (17,000 acres). *Prop.*—Trustees of late W. E. Gilmour. Lessee—M. H. Soames.

A3

GLENCARRON AND GLENUAIG (14,573 acres. *Prop.*—Lady Evelyn Cobbold. Average—45 Stags. Illustrations section shows the last Stag of season 1924 (shot by proprietrix), also photo of Grant, the head stalker, bringing home 5 Hinds shot in deep snow, slid down to the road. and taken home by small 2-seater Calcott.

LADY COBBOLD WITH A ROYAL.

GLENSHIELDAIG (14,467 acres). *Prop.*—Chas. J. Murray of Lochcarron.

GRUINARD (12,912 acres). *Prop.*—Sir Alexander Gibb.

GRIMERSTA. *Prop.*—Sir Jas. Calder.

INCHBAE, BY GARVE (21,000 acres). *Prop.*—Wm. Dalziel Mackenzie, Esq., of Farr, etc., Henley-on-Thames.—Lessees—Lodge and part of Forest —Henry T. L. Young ,Esq., 9a Wilbraham Place, London, S.W. 1 (season 1925). Part of Forest—J. C. Williams, Esq., Caerhays Castle, Gorran, R.S.O., Cornwall (let on lease for 5 years from 1st February, 1925). Average 50 Stags. The northern part of the Forest contains two small plantations in which are some Japanese and Fallow Deer. There is a well-sheltered sanctuary about two miles long. Length of Forest about 14 miles, and width 4 to 5. Narrow at Lodge. Bounded on all sides by forests. In addition to Deer,

Grouse, Black Game, Woodcock, and Ptarmigan are found. Good Salmon and Trout fishing on River Blackwater, and Trout fishing on several good lochs and streams in the Forest. Agents—Innes & Mackay, Inverness.

INVEREWE AND KERNSARY (5,354 acres). *Propx.*—Mrs Robert Hanbury, Inverewe, Poolewe. Lessee—T. A. Hardcastle, Lyndhurst, Hants. Average —25 Stags.

INVERPOLLY (8,698 acres). *Prop.*—The Countess of Cromartie. Lessees— Capt. D. A and W. Lawson.

KILDERMORIE (18,461 acres). *Prop.*—Ardross Estates Co. Lessee—G. S. Albright.

KILLILAN, GLOMACH AND PART OF CORRYEACH (31,000 acres). *Prop.*— W. Melville Wills, Leigh Woods, Bristol. Average—70 Stags and 70 Hinds. Shot over by proprietor since he purchased, in 1914. A number of new roads are being constructed with purely local labour, and water power utilised for electricity. One of the several hills in the Forests reaches a height of 3,770 ft.

KINLOCHEWE (41,000 acres). *Prop.*—Edward Hickman, Danes Court, Wolverhampton. Average—90 Stags. Agents—Dundas & Wilson, C.S., Edinburgh.

KINTAIL AND NORTH CLUANIE (26,495 acres). *Prop.*—Alexander Edward of Sanquhar.

LECKMELM (6,451 acres). *Prop.*—Major J. W. Fraser. Lessees—Mrs de Calry, Frank Cameron.

LEDGOWAN (8,122 acres). *Prop.*—Major Robert Ross.

LETTEREWE AND FISHERFIELD (41,434 acres). *Prop.*—The Earl of Ronaldshay.

LOCHLUICHART (24,345 acres). *Prop.*—The Marquess of Northampton.

LOCHROSQUE (12,864 acres). *Prop.*—John M. MacDonald. Lessee— Major Bertram Hardy.

MONAR (25,000 acres). *Prop.*—Capt. John Stirling, Fairburn, Muir of Ord. Average—40 Stags.

MORSGAIL (15,811 acres). *Prop.*—Lewis & Harris Welfare & Development Co., Ltd, Tarbert, Harris. Average—30 Stags, 20 Hinds, including several Royals. The Morsgail shootings and fishings provide good sport for the months of July, August, September, and October. Salmon are to be got within 100 yards of the Lodge. Agent—Norman Robertson, Tarbert.

PARK (40,656 acres). *Prop.*—Lewis and Harris Welfare Development Co., Ltd. Lessee—Mrs J. A. Platt.

PATT AND RIOCHAN (7,987 acres). *Prop.*—Lt.-Col. Oliver Haig of Ramornie.

RHIDORROCH (18,749 acres). *Prop.*—Sir John Barclay Ross.

SCATWELL AND CABAAN (9,000 acres). *Prop.*—Sir William Cross, Bart., of Scatwell, Muir of Ord. Average—35 Stags. Some good Hinds got. Agent—John Houston, Scatwell Estate Office, Muir of Ord.

SHIELDAIG (8,293 acres). *Prop.*—Sir Kenneth Mackenzie, Bart. Lessee—Major Dugdale.

STRATHGARVE. *Prop.*—Major A. Stirling.

STRATHCONON (60,000 acres). *Prop.*—Captain Christian Combe. Average—100 to 150 Stags.

STRATHVAICH AND TOLMUICK (24,240 acres). *Prop.*—Col. A. F. Mackenzie of Ord, The Countess of Cromartie, and Sir Arthur MacKenzie, Bart., of Coul. Lessee—J. C. Williams.

TORRIDON (17,000 acres). *Prop.*—Lord Woolavington, Lavington Park, Petworth, Sussex. Average—35 Stags.

VIEWFIELD AND INVEROYKEL. *Prop.*—Trustees of late W. E. Gilmour. Lessee—Capt. Kennard, R.N.

WYVIS (26,035 acres). *Prop.*—Col. Rupert Shoolbred.

SUTHERLANDSHIRE.

BADANLOCH (22,205 acres). *Prop.*—The Duke of Sutherland. Lessee—Mrs J. L. Wood.

BEN HEE AND CORRIEKINLOCH (32,000 acres). *Prop.*—A. S. Garton, Loch Merkland, Lairg, and Wood Lodge, Burgh Heath, Surrey. Average—40 Stags. Agents—A. N. Macaulay & Co., Golspie, Sutherland.

DUNROBIN (11,404 acres). *Prop.*—The Duke of Sutherland.

FIAG (8,477 acres). *Prop.*—Wm. Holzapfel. Lessee—Mr Cameron.

GARVAULT (9,410 acres). *Prop.*—W. H. Midwood.

GLENCANNISP (30,000 acres). *Prop.*—Major-General J. Stewart, C.B., C.M.G., of Assynt. Average—40 Stags. Some good Royals, 14-pointers and 11-pointers got.

GOBERNUISGACH (12,325 acres). *Prop.*—Samuel Wilson, Esq., Gobernuisgach, Lairg. and Fulwell West House, Sunderland, Co. Durham. Average—35 Stags, 25 brace Grouse, 20 Woodcock.

INCHNADAMPH (22,000 acres). *Prop.*—Major-General J. Stewart, C.B., C.M.G., of Assynt. Average—30 Stags. Agent—M. Kerr, Factor, Assynt Estate Office, Lochinver.

KILDONAN (2,496 acres). *Prop.*—Brig.-Gen. T. E. Hickman. Lessees—Miss Radcliffe, Col. Sir C. Burn, Bart.

KINLOCH (28,896 acres). *Prop.*—Alexander Morrison. Lessee—Sydney Loder. Average—40 Stags, 50 brace Grouse. Agents—Dove, Lockhart & Smart, Edinburgh.

KINLOCHBERVIE (35,600 acres), part of KEOLDALE (15,000 acres)—50,600 acres. *Prop.*—Brig.-General R. S. Stronach, Kinlochbervie, N.B. Rod fishing bag 1924—75 Salmon (581 lb.), 6 Grilse (27 lb.), 544 Sea Trout (688 lb.), 941 Brown Trout (447 lb.). The above on all waters on the estate. Agent—P. Grant, Bridge Cottage, Kinlochbervie.

LOCH ASSYNT (15,092 acres). *Prop.*—Major-General J. Stewart, C.B., C.M.G., of Assynt. Average—24 Stags. In 1924 bag included 1 fourteen-pointer, 3 Royals, and 3 eleven-pointers. Heaviest, 18 st. 4 lb. Agent—M. Kerr, factor, Assynt, Estate Office, Lochinver.

LOCH CHOIRE, BEN ARMINE, AND DALNESSIE (64,339 acres). *Prop.*—The Duke of Sutherland.

LOCHSIDE AND GRIAMACHORRY (13,680 acres). *Prop.*—F. G. Nutting.

MUDALE (20,812 acres). *Prop.*—Sir L. R. Phillips, Bart.

REAY (76,809 acres). *Prop.*—The Duke of Westminster.

SKINSDALE, BORROBOL (3,936 acres). *Prop.*—Major Alex. Lawson, Annfield, Kingskettle, Fife. Average—30 Stags and 30 Hinds. Best head, 13-pointer, 36 in. wide, shot 1906 (very good), killed by Mr Frank Sykes. Skinsdale shot together with Borrobol, total acres 21,000, marches with His Grace The Duke of Sutherland's Forest.

Lightning Source UK Ltd.
Milton Keynes UK
UKHW051544111218
333825UK00003B/207/P